HOW GIRLS THRIVE

An Essential Guide for Educators (and Parents)

By JoAnn Deak, Ph.D.

© 1998 National Association of Independent Schools
All rights reserved.
Designed by Musikar Design, Rockville, Maryland.
Printed in USA.
ISBN 0-934338-93-0

Front cover photo by Peter Howard, Salem Academy, North Carolina
Back cover photo by Andrew M. Wilson, The Grier School, Pennsylvania
Chapter photos courtesy of Laurel School, Ohio

ACKNOWLEDGMENTS

This book would not have been written without the vision, perseverance, and hard work of Dory Adams as the first NAIS editor. Thanks, also, to Michael Brosnan for those all-important final editorial touches. In addition, no acknowledgment is complete without mentioning the support of family and friends. This small but powerful group gives me the sustenance to take on life, as well as projects like this.

Thank you Mom, Duke, Jeanne...

FOREWORD

This well-written book instructs with stories from professional experiences. It sparkles from conceptual clarity. JoAnn Deak begins with a no-nonsense summary of research on gender issues. This is an enormous and complex area, and her coverage is easy to read and useful. She then offers us good original thinking on the much muddied concept of self-esteem. Her ideas are both theoretical and practical and are presented in ways that have implications for actions. In fact, one of the best things about this book is its recommendations for immediate practical steps in our school systems.

JoAnn Deak is an earnest idealist and a rigorous researcher and critic. She's a good combination of head and heart, of school administrator and writer. I recommend this book to all educators (and even parents) who want to improve the world for girls.

Mary Pipher
Lincoln, Nebraska

PREFACE

"If I waited for perfection... I would never write a word."

— *Margaret Atwood*

For the past ten years, the field of educational and psychological research has focused more on female development than ever before. Some attribute the beginning of this attention to Myra Sadker's and Nancy Frazier's work in the 1960s which culminated in their 1973 book, *Sexism in School and Society*. Other works followed, but it was Carol Gilligan and her study of adolescent females that penetrated the popular press and seemed to be the wake-up call for researchers to study seriously the development of females. Gilligan's book, *In a Different Voice*, sold more copies than any other publication of the Harvard University Press (before or since its publication). From that point on, work in gender research, theory, and opinion has proliferated at a remarkable rate.

Gilligan's work made it clear that, prior to the last two decades, the study of human development was really the study of male development. It is only a natural swing of the pendulum, then, that has caused the research to be skewed, at least in terms of volume, in the direction of the female gender in the 1980s and 1990s — to compensate for the dearth of work in this area prior to this time. Perhaps in the near future the pendulum may settle somewhere in the middle, with equitable focus on males and females. Until that time, there is no need to be apologetic that writings on gender, like this one, focus predominantly on females. In fact, I believe it is utterly necessary.

A review of the literature provides strong evidence that there is not an equal playing field in our schools, that females are "short-changed," as Myra and David Sadker term it. This point of view has not been countermanded by any of the recent research. Although there are certainly backlash articles and books published by such authors as Diane Ravitch and Christina Hoff-Sommers, these publications are opinions about the current research, but do not contain any research studies of their own.

This book is not designed to make the case that pervasive gender inequity exists; so much has been written about that already. The real need now, expressed by school personnel, is to figure out what can we do to facilitate learning and growth equitably for girls and boys.

Although administrators and teachers are becoming more aware of gender issues (one regional association of independent schools requires member schools to include assessment of gender issues in every school evaluation), there still appears to be a great deal of confusion about what the next steps should be. First of all, how does a school analyze gender equity with enough specificity to allow it to set priorities for action? Second, if this can be done, how do you move to selecting those strategies, in a comprehensive way, that will ameliorate gender issues? For instance, if teachers are trained to employ the technique of "wait time" before allowing student responses (a technique that Catherine Krupnick at Harvard, as well as others, have found to increase female participation significantly), will this be enough to increase the performance, self-esteem, and continual participation of girls in this class? And, is this piecemeal approach of selecting splinter techniques really going to affect systemic change in an institution? Also, what happens if some teachers apply gender-fair techniques and others do not?

In short, when it comes to gender equity, there still remains a critical gap between what we profess and what occurs. Schools need a clear way of looking at the entire school, a division of a school, or a class in a school to analyze the gender issues and inequities. And once that holistic and subsequent specific assessment is completed, we need a way of looking at some practices and programs which would match the needs to the most effective changes. This book is designed to help on both accounts.

To provide the reader with the foundation of literature that delineates the issues of gender — to remind us of where we came from and where we need to go — the first chapter is designed to organize the massive amount of data, especially that of the last decade, into a brief, manageable summary. The second chapter sharpens the focus and delineates the external and internal obstacles to girls succeeding in school. Having done that, it will become clear that the thorniest impediment of equity for females is low self-esteem. Therefore, before discussing some practical strategies for change, chapter three is devoted to an in-depth analysis of self-esteem. This concept (often maligned in popular literature) needs to be understood clearly before attempting to change an environment or to influence the humans in that environment. In a way, it is at the heart of all our efforts to make schools more equitable places. The final chapter extends this notion of building the self-esteem of girls by looking at what I call "crucible events" and "crucible moments" in the lives of girls. How we respond to girls in these moments and during these events can go a long way in strengthening their self-esteem. While this book is directed mainly at teachers and school administrators, it is also intended for parents (who, after all, are key educators in the lives of children). This is especially true of the last two chapters — where the advice, based on the best of current research, will go a long way in helping all educators bring out the best in girls.

At this point, some caveats are in order. Of necessity, there will be generalizations made which are meant to convey trends that can be inferred from the literature in this field. It is also clear that there are exceptions to these general statements. However, it would be a mistake to reject a meaningful trend because you may think of an exception to it. As my grandmother used to say, "Don't throw out the baby with the bathwater!" Also, there is little research that is representative of classic research designs with control groups and statistical analyses. It is certainly needed, but it will be the work of the next century. We can't wait to act: educators must be effective and responsive to the needs of females (and males) that exist in our schools now. The book *Failing at Fairness: How America's Schools Cheat Girls* impresses on its readers this imperative for change.

My hope is that this book will help schools begin the process of change— and continue working until we've transformed our schools into more equitable learning environments.

So, with that rationale, let's begin.

CHAPTER ONE

GENDER RESEARCH AND THEORY, WHAT DOES IT SAY?

"Don't confuse me with the facts."
— *Connie Francis*

I f you go to the library and complete a computer search with the key words gender, female, education, development, pedagogy, or any combination of the above, you will be left with a staggering bibliography. Also, you will note a trend: the quantity of writing has increased almost geometrically each year since 1980, or to be conservative, since 1985. More books, articles, and journals appear each day. Gender has become one of the "in" terms in our field.

One way of organizing the gender literature in an efficient manner is to condense it into major themes or categories. For our purposes, the framework will be:

I. Physiological Research and Literature
   A. Developmental
   B. Hormonal
   C. Cognitive

II. Psychological Research and Literature
   A. Self-Esteem
   B. Values/ Morality
   C. Affect

III. Educational Research and Literature
   A. School Structure
   B. Classroom Structure

This chapter summarizes each area and makes connections to our work as educators. Please keep in mind, as with all other areas of education, there is no truth — only perception, opinion, judgment, and common sense. Therefore, each summary will present the material and conclusions from the standpoint of "what a reasonable person would conclude after reading all of this stuff."

I. Physiological Research and Literature

Developmental: Through adolescence, girls mature faster than boys in areas traditionally related to school.

Much of the developmental literature is based on observation and/or theory. For example, first-grade teachers know that, in general, boys' auditory discrimination of short vowel sounds develops at a later age than that skill in girls. Teachers of physical education agree that boys gross motor skills development generally precedes that of girls by a perceptible margin. A kindergarten teacher in an all-boys' school will move into reading-related activities according to a different time-line and will use different techniques than a kindergarten teacher in an all-girls' classroom. The literature supports the position that boys with summer birthdays are more at risk for academic problems in the primary grades than girls with like birthdays. Some of the more recent research focusing at hormonal and neurological factors correlates to these observed differences in growth time-lines by gender.

Hormonal: In the last three to five years, research on the hormonal influences on gender has become clearer. Male and female hormones have a direct impact on the architecture of the brain and, therefore, on the emotional and perceptual systems.

A prolific researcher in this field is Doreen Kimura at the University of Western Ontario. Similar work has been done at the University of Chicago Medical School. A simple summary of this vast body of data is that estrogen and androgen, both in utero and throughout life, have a significant differential physiological affect on humans. Much current work is being done to show the hormonal effects as they pertain to thinking and to behavior. Although far from definitive, this research supports that hormonal input of androgens (e.g. testosterone) in males and estrogen in females cause structural and functional neurologic differences by gender. An example is the CAH (congenital adrenal hyperplasia) girls studied at the Chicago Medical School. These are females who received more testosterone in their systems in utero than a control group of sisters. Measurable hormonal differences in the CAH females is correlated with concomitant differences in behavior and thinking patterns and skills. CAH females play more sports, play with more action-oriented toys, and show a higher level of competence in spatial skills than their estrogen normal sisters. These behaviors are patterns seen in males with normal amounts of testosterone.

The above work suggests that females and males come into the world somewhat programmed, are at least predisposed to certain behavioral and cognitive styles. The world then exacerbates or ameliorates those gender differences, although not always with the same degree of ease. For example, the tendency of young males towards more aggressive play can be greatly enhanced by watching cartoons of action heroes, playing with toy weapons, being reinforced for being tough, etc. However, as most mothers and teachers can attest, the obverse often is not as simple. One anecdote clearly illustrates this point. A previous teacher at my school enrolled her four-year-old son in our preschool. She had been careful, since his birth, to give him a diverse array of toys, including those that would be labeled stereotypically female and stereotypically male. Being a serious pacifist, the latter excluded any form of play weapons or violent games or toys. His television watching and book reading had been chosen with the same care and underlying philosophy. On one unforgettable day, his class was having graham crackers for a snack. This carefully raised boy took the opportunity to bite his graham cracker into the shape of a gun and proceeded to "kill" everyone in the class!

Cognitive: Now that more sophisticated physiological tests are available, the structural and functional cognitive differences between males and females are clear.

An entire issue of *Newsweek* (March 27, 1995) was devoted to the topic of the cognitive difference between males and females. Color pictures of male and female brains showed varying patterns by gender as males and females tried to solve the same problem. This mapping of the neurological circuitry shows that most females use many areas of the brain simultaneously to solve a problem while males tend to use far fewer areas of the brain for the same problem. This work supports the experience of the medical profession which sees more catastrophic results of localized cerebral hemorrhages for males than females. The theory is that females have alternative areas of the brain that they have been using, whereas the males have a more narrow neurological usage pattern, and thus no provision for the compensation of a particular damaged region.

Other cognitive research shows gender differences, also. Keith E. Beery and Norman A. Buktenica, in their work on visual motor development, showed that females develop their fine motor skills at an earlier age than males. When they developed their widely used test, *The Visual Motor Inventory*, Beery and Buktenica provided standard scoring tables by gender and age to reflect the developmental differences they observed.

Although research is documenting the differences between genders, there is also diversity within each gender, which partially accounts for the differing opinions of practitioners as well as for some ambiguous and contradictory research findings. The literature focusing on hormonal and cognitive structural differences between heterosexual and homosexual humans is showing some promise of helping to clarify these gender differences.

In summary, the research and literature focusing on physiological differences between females and males is becoming clearer. Although there is much to be done to refine the data and our understanding of these differences, it is clear that there are physiological differences resulting in gender differences in behavior and cognition.

For more information, see the resources on "Brain Research" at the end of this chapter.

II. Psychological Research and Literature

Self-Esteem: Self-esteem is a critical element in a child's performance, behavior, and the ability to make choices; inequity in the treatment of females is a key factor in the loss of self-esteem.

So much has been written on this topic. Therefore, the focus here will be on the recent research which looks at self-esteem in relation to gender and gender differences. Please note that the terms "self-concept" and "self-esteem" are often used interchangeably in the literature. For reasons that will become clearer in chapter two, the preferred usage in this book will be "self-esteem."

Because it was published pervasively in the popular press, the A.A.U.W. study, as it has been labeled, is the best known representative research in this area. In 1991, this study was sponsored by the American Association of University Women. It included 3,000 schoolchildren between grades four and ten (a detailed account can be obtained from sources in the bibliography). Responses of the girls and boys were shown in various charts with percentages by gender. The data led the researchers to several conclusions, all of which show patterns that are more negative for girls at all ages than for boys. One important pattern was that girls rated their self-esteem significantly lower than boys did theirs. This gap increased as the age of the children moved towards adolescence. The second powerful pattern was that self-esteem had a much more direct effect on behavior for girls than it did for boys. For example, a girl who thinks she is not good in a particular subject — math or science, for instance — will not take an advanced placement course in this area. This correlation does not hold true for boys.

On a par with the media attention given to the above work is the research of Carol Gilligan, Lyn Brown, et al. This group of researchers from Harvard spent years completing longitudinal studies of girls at the Emma Willard School (New York) and Laurel School (Ohio). The findings are complex and multitudinous (many primary resources are available in the bibliography). However, in the area of self-esteem, the Gilligan work is supportive of the data and findings of the A.A.U.W. research.

Gilligan is well known for her writings about the pattern of girls' deteriorating self-esteem resulting in their "loss of voice" by the time they reach adolescence. In the book *Meeting at the Crossroads,* several poignant interviews show the change in girls over time. There is the self-confident second grader who literally blows a whistle at the dinner table because she isn't being heard, contrasted with the senior who jeopardizes her life by riding with a drunk driver rather than saying anything. All of the stories of girls in the ten years between the whistle and the ride show a constant progression of increasing self-doubt and subsequent deterioration of self-esteem. When Gilligan first presented this work at a symposium in Cleveland, an audible gasp went up from the women in the room as they recognized themselves in her stories.

Additional data supporting lower self-esteem in girls comes from more traditional psychological research such as experiments done with younger children around risk-taking. In one study, children were asked to decide for themselves how far from the peg they would stand in a ring toss game. Most boys chose to stand a good distance away, as if compelled by the risk. Girls, meanwhile, chose to stand very close, almost guaranteeing their success. While this study, in and of itself, does not prove that girls have lower self-esteem than boys, the accumulation of studies with this kind of gender differential provides a mountain of circumstantial evidence that is hard to ignore.

Values/Morality: The literature supports the existence of differing views and beliefs by gender. Females often use a lens of connectedness while males usually choose a lens of justice for their decision-making.

Like self-esteem, values and morality have been the subject of much thought, research, and voluminous publications. However, until Carol Gilligan's 1982 publication of *In a Different Voice,* a comprehensive description, let alone study, of female moral development had not been done. All of the work of major developmentalists like Jean Piaget and Erik Erikson had focused on male development. Likewise, the moral developmentalists, with Lawrence Kohlberg as the most recent and well known, used only males in their studies and then generalized the findings to all human development. Gilligan's studies of female development have been criticized (subjective, the critics charge) because they are dependent on anecdotal accounts that have been coded by her research affiliates. However, thousands of women and girls who have participated in or read Gilligan's research find that their own sense of morality resonates with these anecdotal accounts.

Simply put, Gilligan's paradigm indicates that males and females hold very different sets of values that result in differing moral priorities, and therefore, judgments, actions, and feelings. According to Gilligan, there are two types of moral orientations. One is labeled justice or fairness; the other is labeled as caring or connectedness. All people possess both orientations, but, like handedness, justice is more dominant in males and connectedness more dominant in females.

The justice point of view identifies things as good or bad based on an accepted framework of fairness — promises should be kept, stealing is bad, there are no exceptions to the following laws, etc. The connectedness point of view is more situational. For example, breaking a promise not to hurt someone's feelings is acceptable, or lying to a teacher to protect a friend is honorable, not a breach of the honor code.

Gilligan and subsequent writers and researchers contend that most laws in society and rules in schools are based on the justice orientation of moral development. This often results in females being penalized or degraded for their moral beliefs or actions — or leaves them feeling out of sync. Some psychologists contend that this is one of the bases for the downward trend in self-esteem as females experience more of the world's consequences and social mores.

The honor codes that exist in many schools are good examples of this difficulty. A typical honor code tenet is that a person who knows of an honor code offense must report it to the appropriate school person or be held as guilty and accountable as the transgressor. In one girls' school that had such an honor code, an "underground" method of dealing with such situations evolved. When someone saw a peer cheat during a test, instead of reporting the infraction, she would either tell a trusted adult in the school community and ask for advice, or tell the transgressor that she had seen what happened and hoped that the girl would not do it again or would "confess" to the appropriate teacher. When these underground paths became evident, many discussions were held with the teachers and the students in the school community. After considering what was happening and reviewing the literature on the moral development of females, the school made several changes in the honor code. Among other things, in essence, the alternatives listed above were legitimized and made a functional and public part of the code.

Affect: The affective system of the brain (also known as the limbic system) is the seat of human emotions. Although the cause is still hotly debated, the literature indicates that females are more significantly influenced than males by the affective system in terms of values, beliefs, and behavior.

Next to the nature/nurture debate, this topic causes the most heated discussions and arguments. The only area of agreement is that we don't know as much as we would like, and a great deal of additional study is necessary. Having said this, many educators and psychologists believe that the affective domain has significant impact on beliefs and behaviors. Experienced coaches, educators, business executives, and the like know that capturing the affective system of individuals or groups can make the difference between success and failure. Leaders from Jesus to Hitler recognized the power of the limbic system (the seat of emotions in the brain) over the cortex (the home of rational thought).

Whether it is a result of nature, nurture, or both, in general, women express, and seem to be influenced by, their feelings more than men are influenced by their feelings. Mary Belenky, et al. devoted a whole book to the topic: *Women's Ways of Knowing.* In an interview with Judy Mann, a popular newspaper columnist and published author, Anne Petersen, the vice president for research at the University of Minnesota, states that females "may be wired to have more social sensitivity," but she is also quick to point out the influence of environmental imperatives.

Most teachers have had the experience of having a girl feel that the teacher does not like her because of the grades she has been given by her teacher. A male physics teachers found that when boys came to him for extra help, they typically just wanted to get down to work and to solve the problem. Girls, however, wanted to discuss how they were feeling about their difficulties and to be reassured by the teacher. The A.A.U.W. study has examples of girls avoiding courses based on affective factors related to grades, while in similar circumstances, many boys attribute their poor grades or failure to a teacher and continue to perform and take courses in that particular subject area or with that particular teacher.

One of the best sources of current research on gender differences in learning is the book *Mathematics and Gender* by Elizabeth Fennema and Gilah Leder. Many of the studies are not related just to the subject of math. Under the topic, "Internal Beliefs," the authors conclude that "affective variables have a more important influence on the achievement and participation of females than they do for males." Mary Belenky takes this data and suggests that teachers who take the affective component seriously and structure their classrooms, styles of teaching, and curriculum around this knowledge are much more successful with girls than teachers who do not take these factors into account. She dubs these teachers, "connected teachers." In addition, the literature surrounding cooperative learning supports this point of view.

III. Educational Research and Literature

School Structure: The research points to structural components of a school or system that can and do influence gender equity. Those reported as positive for girls include single-gender settings that are democratic and collaborative.

One of the clearest areas of research in the last several years is the area of single-gender learning environments. Whether it is single-gender schools, single-gender classes within coeducational schools, or single-gender groupings of students within coeducational classes, the research supports these structures as being quite positive for females. Girls in these situations, in general, get better grades, report that they learn more and are more positive about the learning situation, have higher self-esteem, and more often move on to advanced courses than do girls in regular coeducational situations.

In 1992, the U.S. Department of Education published a summary of the last twenty years of research on single-gender versus coeducational schools. The general conclusion was that all of the studies supported single-gender schools as better learning environments for girls.

Classroom Structures: Research dramatically supports single-gender classes, especially in middle and high schools.

The data on single-gender classes in coeducational schools is just as dramatic as the data for single-gender schools. Most of the classes have been at the middle or upper school level and in the areas of math or science. Also, most attempts at creating single-gender classes in coeducational schools have occurred in the independent school world, although several public school districts have made attempts in this area recently (e.g. The Leadership School in New York City and, more recently, a handful of schools in California). However, in the public sector, the school systems are open to charges of discrimination by the American Civil Liberties Union. This action has had a pervasive and curtailing effect on public school efforts in this area.

Nevertheless, the reports about all-girls classes in both public and private schools, and a recent survey of such schools, indicates that these classes have proven successful. School personnel reported significant positive results for girls participating in the single-gender classes.

"It was one of the most positive changes we have ever made," said Joan Lutton, head of The Cushman School (Florida). "The girls self-images rose immediately." When asked for words of wisdom for schools contemplating the creation of single-gender classes, Nancy Calhoun, middle school head at The Walker School (Georgia), said, "Do it!" She went on to say that "girls, at first, overwhelmed the teachers with questions. They were so enthusiastic they voluntarily asked for and attended after-school sessions. Their achievement was truly impressive." Pam Belitski, seventh-grade math teacher at the

Anacapa Middle School (California), added, "The classroom atmosphere is more productive...girls are aggressively exploring with manipulatives, measuring, and problem solving, and becoming divergent thinkers. This school year the girls' math class has increased three times from its original size."

Another interesting report came from Catherine C. Veal, director of communications, Illinois Mathematics and Science Academy (Illinois). "Students in the all-female class," she said, "displayed greater performance-level growth on quizzes, homework, and class exams than did females in the coeducational section taught by the same teacher.... More females enrolled in and successfully completed Calculus-Based Physics than ever before. There was a strikingly different quality to the atmosphere, character, and climate of the all-female class. The learning community that emerged was characterized by a profound sense of responsibility for learning, a special rapport between and among the teacher and the students, a spirit of co-learning, with both the teacher and the students feeling free to ask questions, admit mistakes, take risks, express confusion, etc."

Other structural and environmental areas are supported by the literature on single-gender schools or single-gender classes literature. Girls perform better and report more satisfaction and confidence in democratic, cooperative, connected, inclusive, hands-on educational settings. Professional groups from the National Council for Teachers of Math (in their recent publication on math standards) to the National Association for the Education of Young Children (in their *Developmentally Appropriate Practices for Young Children*) to the Association for School Curriculum Development (in their annual report on curricular research) all support the above structures for girls, as well as boys, in most situations.

A few qualifiers are in order. Competition seems to work well for boys and a minority of girls and should not be deleted totally from the educational world. Likewise authoritarian, directed teaching is useful and effective in instances of advanced placement courses, preparing for information-based exams, etc. In addition, teaching splinter skills absent from meaningful integration or understanding is useful for students who have a particular learning disability or low

aptitude in a particular area. In other words, all educational structures and pedagogical techniques have their place. The difficult
part is knowing when to impose which structure and when to use
a particular technique based on the group or individual needs of
the learners. This is why teachers should earn more money than
pitchers on professional baseball teams! The needs of individual
learners or differing learning styles compel us to maintain a huge
array of pedagogical arrows in our educational quivers.

*For more information, see the resources on "Single-Gender Education"
at the end of this chapter.*

Curriculum: What textbooks are used, what is taught, and the equity and inclusiveness of the curriculum, all influence learners.

Peggy Macintosh, at Wellesley College, is the recognized guru in
this area. Please consult her and say that I sent you! Seriously, much
work has been done at the Wellesley Center for Research on Women
and Girls and many other colleges and universities. It is not very
profound to say that females feel disconnected when courses are all
about wars and male achievements, or that male-oriented language
(e.g. the generic "mankind" for "humankind") has a deleterious effect
on readers or that learning is more meaningful when it is related to
something meaningful in the learner's world. Not very profound,
but also not very well adhered to in the educational world. It is one
area that can be analyzed clearly by looking at texts and materials
to make them inclusive, fair, and meaningful. In this area, one of
the best sources of thought and suggestions is Anne Chapman's new
book, *A Great Balancing Act: Equitable Education for Girls and Boys*,
published by the National Association of Independent Schools.

Pedagogy: How each teacher teaches influences the learning and interaction in the classroom. Some techniques are gender fair, others are not. Those techniques that the research supports as positive for girls are not negative for boys.

Much of this has been implied in the above sections. In terms of
relevance to gender, there are three areas of clear focus in the literature: air time, modeling/mentoring, and hands-on experience.

Air Time

The first area of pedagogy to consider is "air time," a term that was derived from the work of researchers who focused, literally, on the air waves of the classroom by observing, videotaping, categorizing, and tallying the interactions in classrooms of various grade levels in various types of schools. This area of research has quite consistent data. For example, in their research, Myra and David Sadker have discovered that in a coeducational setting girls, compared with boys, are:

■ five times less likely to receive the most attention from teachers

■ three times less likely to be praised

■ eight times less likely to call out in class

■ three times less talkative in class

■ half as likely to demand help or attention

■ half as likely to be called on in class

The conclusions seem to be incontrovertible: in general boys talk more, move more, have their hands up more, do more, argue more, get more of the teachers' attention than do girls in a coeducational setting. One of the best illustrative vignettes is the short segment that appeared on the television program *Sixty Minutes* in 1994. There are incredible scenes with kindergarten boys moving from the back to the front of the classroom to be near and to talk with the adult reader, blocking the view of the children (mostly girls) who are now in the back of the room. One shot of a middle school classroom pans the room when a question is asked and shows the abundance of male hands and a dearth of female hands in the air. An interview of several high school girls confirms that this unequal air time exists in the upper grades also.

Two questions immediately come to mind when one reads these conclusions. First, why is this so? And, second, why does it matter? Unfortunately, research rarely answers why questions. Almost any research is correlational, not causal. To prove causation requires a rigorous and rigid research design with control groups. One group receives one "treatment," e.g. spelling workbooks; one group receives another "treatment," e.g. whole language literature books; and one group receives no "treatment," that is, does not focus on spelling at all. You can see that this paradigm would not be acceptable under most circumstances in the educational world, because the "no treatment" control group needs to be there to prove that improvement in spelling is not the result of natural growth and development. Few schools, teachers, parents, or students would allow a control group to receive no treatment regardless of how important it could be in making conclusions about pedagogy and learning.

So, the long-winded answer to the question of why "air time" is skewed in favor of boys is: We do not know for certain. The single-gender schools and classes literature, however, does provide some plausible answers. Girls report that boys are louder, talk without thinking, make fun of girls' answers, etc. The U.S. Department of Education's report on single-gender versus coeducational schools included evidence of the above. When trying to look at the variables which contributed to the repressive effect of coeducational environments on girls, Diane Ravitch, the author of the report, stated that no single variable could be identified. However, it was clear that the mere presence of boys was a critical factor in this suppressive effect on girls' performance and attitude.

Catherine Krupnick, of Harvard University, and many other teacher trainers, suggest a variety of methods for reducing the imbalance of air time in schools. These include such techniques as:

- ■ waiting five seconds before allowing anyone to answer a question posed

- ■ having students write down key words for their response before they respond orally to a discussion/question

- ■ repeating the previous person's response before giving a response

- equity techniques such as giving each student three chips to "spend" during a class — everyone has to talk three times — no more, no less

- putting students into small groups

- arranging the seating so that all of the talkers are not clustered together

- structuring tasks so that everyone has a task, question, topic to share with the class

- encouraging the students to keep response tallies for a period of time to help with decisions about "air" equity in the classroom

- literally taking turns — a boy's response, then a girl's response...

- establish rules of discourse, such as "you may not put down anyone's answers"

This list could continue, but the gist is clear. If there are not constraints, structures, or guidelines in coeducational classrooms of all ages, the research clearly shows that the imbalance of air time is in favor of the boys with about 70 percent of teacher-student interactions, and only 30 percent of the interactions being between the teacher and the girls. Regardless of the causation, experience shows that the imbalance can be countermanded by a variety of not-so-difficult-to-employ techniques and the increased awareness of the key players: teachers and students. However, a warning is needed here: in classrooms where teachers have altered their behavior in the direction of parity, both boys and girls become uncomfortable and complain of unfairness when the level of interaction drops to about 60 percent with the boys and rises to about 40 percent with the girls. It should also be noted that even in the classroom where all of the above techniques are used, it is very difficult to get some students to participate. The thorny problem of how to get girls with low self-esteem to talk will be covered in a later chapter.

Modeling/Mentoring

A second area of pedagogy is the use of modeling and mentoring. Studies in this area have demonstrated that while a brief contact with a model/mentor (such as a career day) can have some impact, the best results come when the connection is sustained over time. In this case, the presence of a mentor can lead to dramatic improvement in the self-esteem and performance of girls.

Deborah Berger in *Parenting Insights* (Issue 10, 1995) writes: "It makes sense that adults — besides parents — can play important, positive roles in children's lives, and there's even research to back this up. The article, *What Kids Need to Succeed: Proven, Practical Ways to Raise Good Kids* (Free Spirit Publishing, 1995) discusses the results of a survey of more than 270,000 young people in 600 communities across the country. The three authors...identified thirty assets that every youngster needs. Number four on the list: having adults, besides parents, who can provide advice and support."

Next to single-gender classes, programs that include mentors and modeling have the most positive impact on the achievement and attitude of girls. "Take Your Daughter to Work Day" is a very public example of this. Reports from girls across the nation appeared in newspapers and were heard in classrooms by teachers the next day. Anna Quindlen, the Pulitzer Prize-winning journalist, tells a great story about her sons. She was driving home one day with her two boys sitting and talking in the back seat. The oldest boy said to the youngest boy, "I want to be a doctor when I grow up." The youngest boy laughed and said, "You can't be a doctor, doctors are girls!" Needless to say, his pediatrician...

Universities are experimenting with all female math and/or science dorms. One of the catalysts for this was the disturbing statistics showing a very high drop-out rate of female science or math majors as they moved to graduate school. This one change has improved those statistics. This sounds like another example of the importance of a single-gender environment, and it is, but that is not all that this program represents. The female graduate students act as mentors and models for each other, and professors often stop in and have discussions with the residents. So this becomes, in essence, a live-in mentoring/modeling experience.

Many middle schools are experimenting with mentoring programs for girls at this critical and fragile developmental stage of life. The Community School in Cleveland, for example, was worried about the drop-out and pregnancy rate of girls from their middle school. They instituted a program which paired each girl with a working adult female. If a girl had a dream about being a veterinarian, her partner was a female veterinarian. Mentors and "mentees" met at school once a month for lunch and the girls made several visits each year to their mentors' places of work. The results were as expected: drop-out and pregnancy rates plummeted, grades improved, girls reported higher levels of self-esteem.

Other programs include:

■ A Duke University Community Initiative
Contact: Mary Wyer, WISE Project Graduate School, North Carolina State University, Box 7102, Raleigh, NC 27695-7102

■ Denver Public Schools Mentoring Program — provided 1,000 high school students with mentors from the Denver business and professional community
Contact: Denver City Schools Board of Education, 900 Grant Street, Room 705, Denver, CO 80203

■ Girls Incorporated Friendly Peersuasion Program — middle school girls work with adult role models and then develop abuse prevention activities to share with girls 6-10
Contact: Girls Incorporated National Resource Center, 441 West Michigan Street, Indianapolis, IN 46202

■ International Women's Writing Guild Mentor Project — designed to match mentors with young women who love to write
Contact: IWWG, P.O. Box 810, Gracie Station, New York, NY 10028

■ Internship program at the Madeira School (Virginia) — provides work placement in the greater Washington, D.C. area for its students
Contact: The Madiera School, 8328 Georgetown Pike, McLean, VA 22101

■ Laurel School Alumnae Pen Pals and Primary Students Program
— connects alumnae of all ages with third and fourth graders
*Contact: JoAnn Deak, Laurel School, 1 Lyman Circle, Shaker Heights,
OH 44122*

■ Math Options — Pennsylvania State University's summer institute
for girls and women to work with university personnel in science
and math
*Contact: Tracey Dolan, Regional Coordinator for Math Options,
Pennsylvania State University, Delaware County Campus, Media, PA
19063*

■ Miss Porter's School/Maria Sanchez Elementary School Big/Little
Sister Program — pairs the older girls of Miss Porter's
(Connecticut) with the younger girls of Maria Sanchez in a one
on one tutoring and mentoring relationship
*Contact: M. Burch Tracy Ford, Head of School, Miss Porter's School, 60
Main Street, Farmington, CT 06032*

■ Simmons College MBA program for women — an intensive one-
year program for women only
*Contact: Margaret Hennig, Simmons Graduate School of Management,
409 Commonwealth Avenue, Boston, MA 02215*

■ WAM — Women and Mathematics is a national network
designed to interest young women in mathematics by providing
role models and mentors
*Contact: Virginia Knight, Department of Mathematics and Computer
Science, Meredith College, Raleigh, NC 27602*

All of the above programs report positive results from the mentor
relationships in their programs.

Doing

The third area of pedagogy to consider is "doing." Don't just talk
about it, read about it, or think about it — *do* it. Whatever the "it"
is, research supports the act of experiencing/doing as key to long-
term effects on the doer.

This area is hard to label, but easy to understand. Projects, labs, building, manipulatives, games, hands-on activities, volunteering are all good options. But, the word "doing" is so nice and clean and simple! There is an old Chinese proverb that says:

> I hear and I forget.
> I see and I remember.
> I do and I understand.

Whatever you call it, research, experience, logic, and common sense all tell us that "doing" is a very effective way of embedding something in our long-term memory banks. All of the many current books on effective teaching/learning for females promote hands on learning as very beneficial for girls.

Air time techniques, modeling and mentors, and hands-on learning are repetitive themes in all of the gender pedagogical research. Please check out the resources on "Critical Reading for Educators" at the end of this chapter. It contains the most recent and comprehensive strategies, techniques, and methods for effective teaching/learning of girls. If you consult these, you will find a wealth of ideas and be considered for the Who's Who of Well Read Professionals in the Field of Gender and Education.

IV. Backlash Literature

In the last few years, the onslaught of research and writing on gender equity, and the heavy coverage of it in the media, has been followed by authors who disagree with this stance. The core of their argument is that the world has changed and inequities no longer exist.

After more than a decade of research focusing on females, their needs and inequities that affect them, several articles appeared that could be called the "You've Come a Long Way, Baby" literature. In other words, the position, simply stated, is that there is no need to talk about unlevel playing fields or how schools cheat girls, since things have changed so much for females recently. The difference between these writings and the literature summarized above is that there is no research contained in these works. The backlash literature is just that, a critical denial of the research of others.

Two leaders in the backlash literature are Diane Ravitch, previous director of the Department of Education under the Bush administration, and Christina Hoff-Sommers, a published psychologist. One of the best and most condensed discussions of this topic appeared in a *New York Times* (February 13, 1994) article written by Catherine S. Manegold. She quotes Diane Ravitch's own words: " 'How can you be a victim when you have succeeded?' Ms. Ravitch asked while calling up a computer file showing female gains in such traditionally male studies as algebra, geometry, and chemistry. 'When do we declare victory? When we are at 60 percent of the college population? When we are at 70 percent?' "

No one contends that there hasn't been dramatic improvement in gender equity, especially in the last decade. Patricia B. Campbell is a director of a research company that evaluates math and science education. A quote from her, in the same *Times* article, rebuts Ravitch: "Look, if you take the number of high school girls who wanted to go into engineering in 1972 and compare that with the figures now, you see a 1,300 percent gain, and that sounds fabulous. But in 1990, boys were still six times more apt than girls to want to go into engineering."

Later in the article, Elizabeth T. Kennan, president of Mount Holyoke College, provides further statistics and comments. "Last year," she writes, "there were 18,000 boys eligible for National Merit Scholarships, and there were only 8,000 girls. So something is happening, and I think it needs to be urgently addressed."

In her book, Christina Hoff-Sommers focuses more on pulling apart the statistics or methods of research. While she does make some valid points about over-generalization from the current research, and the need for more causal research, she is not able to cite any research that contradicts the massive amount of research that she attacks.

In short, the backlash literature focuses on two points: things are much better for females now, and some of the research is flawed. Both arguments have some veracity to them. However, the gender research summarized earlier clearly shows that there is much more that needs to be done in terms of gender equity in education and that there is presently no contradictory research. The experience and daily observations of most educators and psychologists who work with girls supports the belief that girls are not being given equal opportunities.

Conclusion

This summary is not meant to be an exhaustive look at the literature but an overview to help educators be more knowledgeable about gender issues. It is hoped that this knowledge base will help in the task of analyzing a system (e.g. school, division, department, or class) and then making decisions about what can be done to create a learning and living environment for all children that is equitable and effective.

Resources

Brain Growth and Development:

Begley, Sharon. "Your Child's Brain." *Newsweek,* February 19, 1996.

"Brain Calisthenics." *Life,* July, 1994.

Fellman, Bruce. "A Tale of Two Brains." *Yale,* Summer 1995.

Hampson, Elizabeth and Doreen Kimura. "Brief Communication: Reciprocal Effects of Hormonal Fluctuations on Human Motor and Perceptual-Spatial Skills." *Behavioral Neuroscience*, Vol. 102, No. 3, 1988.

"In Search of the Mind." *Time,* July 17, 1995.

Kerr, Barbara A. *Smart Girls Two: A New Psychology of Girls, Women and Giftedness.* Dayton, Ohio: Ohio Psychology Press, 1994.

Kimura, Doreen. "Are Men's and Women's Brains Really Different?" *Canadian Psychology* (1987), 28:2.
___"Cognitive Function: Sex Differences and Hormonal Influences." *Neuroscience Year: Supplement 2 to the Encyclopedia of Neuroscience.* Birkhauser Boston, 1992.
___"How Different Are Male and Female Brains?" *Orbit,* Published by Ontario Institute for Studies in Education, Vol. 17, No. 3 (October, 1986).

_____"Monthly Fluctuations in Sex Hormones Affect Women's Cognitive Skills." *Psychology Today,* November, 1989.

_____"Sex Differences, Human Brain Organization." *Encyclopedia of Neuroscience,* Vol. II, 1987.

"Mind and Brain." *Scientific American, Special Issue,* Vol. 267, No. 3, September, 1992.

Swerdlow, Joel L. "Quiet Miracles of the Brain." *National Geographic,* Vol. 187, No. 6, June 1995.

Sylwester, Robert. *A Celebration of Neurons: An Educator's Guide to the Brain.* Alexandria, Virginia: Association for Supervision and Curriculum Development, 1995.

"The New Science of the Brain." *Newsweek,* March 27, 1995.

Watson, Neil V. and Doreen Kimura. "Nontrivial Sex Differences in Throwing and Intercepting: Relation to Psychometrically-Defined Spatial Functions." *Personality and Individual Differences,* Vol. 12, No. 5, 1991.

Single-Gender Education:

Hollinger, Debra and Rebecca Adamson, eds., "Single-Sex Schooling: Proponents Speak." *Vol. II, A Special Report from the Office of Educational Research and Improvement,* U.S. Department of Education, 1992.

"Issues Involving Single-Gender Schools and Programs." *A Report to the Chairman*, Committee on the Budget, House of Representatives, May 1996.

Lawton, Millicent. "Bias Against Girls Found in Both Coed, One-Sex Schools." *Education Week,* June 10, 1992.

Riordan, Cornelius. *Girls and Boys in School: Together or Separate?* New York: Teachers College, Columbia University, 1990.

Sedgwick, John. "What Difference Does a Single Sex School Make to a Girl Later in Life?" *Self Magazine*, March 1997.

"Single-Sex Schooling: Perspectives from Practice and Research." *Vol. I, A Special Report from the Office of Educational Research and Improvement.* U.S. Department of Education, 1992.

"Boys and Girls: Together and Apart." *Independent School,* Fall 1992.

Critical Readings for Educators:

Achieving Gender Equity in the Classroom and on the Campus: The Next Steps. American Association of University Women, 1995.

Barrs, Myra and Sue Pidgeon. *Reading the Difference: Gender and Reading in Elementary Classrooms.* Maine: Stenhouse Publishers, 1993.

Bogart, Karen. *Solutions that Work: Identification and Elimination of Barriers to the Participation of Female and Minority Students in Academic Educational Programs.* Professional Standards and Practice, National Education Association.

Brandt, Ronald S. *Cooperative Learning and the Collaborative School.* Virginia: Association of Supervision and Curriculum Development, 1991.

Butler, Kathleen A. *Learning Styles: Personal Exploration and Practical Applications.* Connecticut: The Learner's Dimension, 1995.

Campbell, Patricia B. *Girls Are... Boys Are... Myths, Stereotypes and Gender Differences.* Newton, Massachusetts: WEEA Resource Center, 1996.

Chapman Anne. *A Great Balancing Act: Equitable Education for Girls and Boys.* Washington, D.C.: National Association of Independent Schools, 1997.

Conwell, Catherine and Kitty B. Cobb, et al. *Science Equals Success.* Massachusetts: WEEA Publishing Center, Education Development Center, Inc., 1990.

Cotera, Martha P. *Checklists for Counteracting Race and Sex Bias in Educational Materials.* Austin, Texas: Women's Educational Equity Act, U.S. Department of Education, 1982.

Countryman, Joan. *Writing to Learn Mathematics: Strategies that Work, K-12.* New Hampshire: Heinemann, 1992.

Downie, Diane et al. *Math for Girls and Other Problem Solvers.* California: EQUALS, University of California, 1981.

Fennema, Elizabeth and Gilah Leder, eds. *Mathematics and Gender.* New York: Teachers College, Columbia University, 1990.

Franklin, Margaret, et al. *Add-Ventures for Girls: Building Math Confidence: Elementary Teacher's Guide.* Massachusetts: WEEA Publishing Center, Education Development Center, 1990.

Gabriel, Susan L. and Isaia Smithson, eds. *Gender in the Classroom: Power and Pedagogy.* Illinois: University of Illinois Press, 1990.

Gaskell, Jane and John Willinsky, eds. *Gender Informs Curriculum*. New York: Teachers College Press, 1995.

"Gender, Language, and Literacy." *Language Arts*. Vol. 70, No. 2, February 1993.

Genshaft, Judy and Jack Naglieri. *A Mindset for Math: Techniques for Identifying and Working with Math-Anxious Girls*. Massachusetts: WEEA Publishing Center Education Development Center, Inc., 1987.

Hansen, Sunny et al. *What's Working for Girls in School*. Washington, D.C.: American Association of University Women Educational Foundation, 1995.

Hanson, Katherine. *Center for Equity and Cultural Diversity Working Paper One: Teaching Mathematics Effectively and Equitably to Females*. Massachusetts: WEEA Publishing Center, Education Development Center, Inc., 1992.

"How to Teach Our Kids." *Newsweek (Special Edition — Education: A Consumer's Handbook)*, Fall/Winter, 1990.

Humphrey, Bernice. *What's Equal: Figuring Out What Works for Girls in Coed Settings*. New York: Girls Inc., 1992.

Leder, Gilah C. "Mathematics and Gender: Changing Perspectives." *Critical Issues*.

Math and Science for Girls: Convening the Experts, Reforming the Classroom, Finding the Right Equation. The National Coalition of Girls' Schools, November, 1992.

Murphy, Susan H. "Closing the Gender Gap: What's Behind the Differences in Test Scores, What Can Be Done About It." *The College Board Review*, No. 163, Spring, 1992, 18-36.

Overholt, Jim. *Math Wise!: Hands-On Activities and Investigations for Elementary Students*. New York: The Center for Applied Research in Education, 1995.

Perl, Teri. *Women and Numbers*. California: Wide World Publishing/Tetra, 1993.

Rosser, Phyllis. *The SAT Gender Gap: Identifying the Causes*. Washington, D.C.: Center for Women Policy Studies, 1989.

Rubin, Donnalee. *Gender Influences: Reading Student Texts*. Illinois: Southern Illinois University Press, 1993.

Sadker, Myra and David. *Failing at Fairness: How America's Schools Cheat Girls.* New York: Charles Scribner's Sons, 1994.

Sanders, Jo. *Lifting the Barriers.* New York: Jo Sanders Publications, 1994.

Sanders, Jo. *The Neuter Computer: Computers for Girls and Boys.* New York: Neal-Schuman Publishers, Inc., 1996.

Smith, Dian G. "Preschools Shortchange Girls." *Sesame Street Parents' Magazine,* September, 1992.

"Strategies for Success: What's Working in Education Today." *Harvard Educational Review,* 1990.

Thorne, Barrie. *Gender Play: Girls and Boys in School.* New Jersey: Rutgers University Press, 1993.

Washington, Mary Ford. *Real Life Math Mysteries: A Kid's Answer to the Question, "What Will We Ever Use This For?"* Texas: Prufrock Press, 1995.

Wheeler, Kathryn. *Special Report: How Schools Can Stop Shortchanging Girls (and Boys): Gender-Equity Strategies: A Practical Manual for K-12 Educators.* Massachusetts: Center for Research on Women, 1993.

Wilbur, Jessica. *Totally Private and Personal: Journaling Ideas for Girls and Young Women.* Minneapolis, Minnesota: Free Spirit Publishing Co., 1996.

Willis, Scott. "Cooperative Learning Shows Staying Power." *Update: Association for Supervision and Curriculum Development,* Vol. 34, No. 3, March, 1992.

Willoughby, Stephen S. *Mathematics Education for a Changing World.* Virginia: The Association for Supervision and Curriculum Development, 1990.

Young, Wathene. *A-Gay-Yah: A Gender Equity Curriculum for Grades 6-12.* Massachusetts: WEEA Publishing Center, Education Development Center, Inc., 1992.

CHAPTER TWO

EXTERNAL
AND INTERNAL
CONSTRAINTS

*"A good idea will keep you awake during the morning,
but a great idea will keep you awake during the night."*

— *Marilyn Van Savant*

The first chapter made it clear that gender imbalances in schools exist and need to be addressed. Yet the process of identifying the areas of gender imbalance, determining the factors involved, and deciding upon strategies for action is very complex. This may explain why even very good schools hesitate to tackle the problem of gender equity in any systematic way. Typically, schools have looked at visible external factors that could or do influence gender equity, such as structure of classes or pedagogical techniques. When external changes are made that yield positive results, the process of change is often considered successful and complete. The most common example is a school that provides gender workshops for their teachers. The teachers then go forth and use equity techniques such as wait time in a discussion class, or more cooperative and team learning. Although the beneficial effects are apparent, they are not enough. There are still those individuals who do not participate in the discussion or the newly formed cooperative group because of internal constraints — low self-esteem being paramount among these.

It is important, therefore, for all schools to carefully examine both the external and internal factors that lead to gender inequity in their communities.

External

Because external constraints are so much easier to identify, schools concerned about gender equity often begin with a numerical collection of data. Usually the data reveals concerns like these:

1) Five out of six major administrators are male.

2) Six varsity sports options are for girls, two for boys.

3) The science faculty is all male.

It is clear that a judgment is being made that numerical imbalances can lead to and/or can cause inequities in the educational opportunities for and/or the treatment of either gender. Although there is no hard data to prove this, experienced educators and the anecdotal reports of students tend to substantiate this claim. For example, girls and their teachers report that girls talk in class far less when there are many more boys than girls. This is an example of the data that comes from the "air time" studies.

Keeping in mind the knowledge about gender and what is beneficial for girls (and boys) as a guiding philosophy, strategies for the above inequities could include:

1) When openings occur, find and hire highly qualified females for administrative positions in the school.

2) Create the same number of varsity opportunities for boys and girls.

3) Bring in outside female speakers for science classes; form an affiliation with a graduate school and provide internships for female science students.

Data collection and analysis helps to identify external factors that contribute to inequity. Each school needs to be flexible and creative in identifying which imbalances are worth correcting based on the data, the school's philosophy and mission, the board's priorities, cost factors, etc. It is conceivable, for instance, that a school would choose not to alter the varsity imbalance if 80 percent of the school body were female. On the other hand, the school may want to identify admission strategies for attracting more male students to the school!

Some numerical imbalances are not controversial and some simple strategies can make immediate and highly visible positive equity changes. However, others are more complicated or controversial, and you then need to identify whether the imbalances are due to external factors, internal factors, or a combination of the two. It may be that strategies can be used which have multiplicative positive effects. Keep reading if this sounds fuzzy; the clouds will part soon.

Let's begin to look at the reasons for imbalances. As noted, external constraints or barriers are often easier to identify. This is somewhat confusing as a term, but, put simply, external constraints are external to the person being constrained. Therefore, a chauvinist teacher's beliefs can be an external constraint to the females in his class (even though his belief system is internal to him!). Some familiar examples of external constraints are:

1) The gymnasium is fully utilized and there are no more periods available to increase the P.E. offerings for girls. The external constraints may be limited space and/or scheduling constraints.

2) Sharing the math faculty between the middle and upper school could ameliorate a male dominated math department in the upper school, but the schedules are different for each division and do not allow cross-over teaching. The external constraint is the different schedules.

3) The teacher uses equal participation discussion techniques, but since there is a 5 to 1 ratio of boys to girls in this class, the girls' participation has not increased. The external constraint is the number of boys and the number of girls. (There may also be internal constraints operating — more about this later).

Removal of the external constraints for the above situations could include:

1a) Offer a P.E. class in another area of the school, e.g. dance in the dance studio. Or use community spaces such as the community swimming pool.

1b) Convince donors of the inequity and build another gym.

2a) Change to an all-school schedule that will allow cross-over teaching.

2b) Retrain teachers and have some upper school teachers become middle school teachers.

3a) Create gender balanced sub-groups for the girls.

3b) Combine with other sections of the class and redistribute according to gender numerical equity.

As you can see by the two alternative suggestions offered for each situation, options for removing or reducing external constraints can differ markedly in difficulty, cost, resistance, and philosophy. There is no easy-to-follow formula which says, "if you find this, then do this." Each school needs to identify the gender issues and respond with actions that fit its system or choose not to act and provide data and justification for that decision. This is a good time to offer a caveat. External constraints are usually in place for one or more reasons. Even though it may make sense or it is the "right" thing to do to remove them, there will be resistance to change.

Resistance always happens when change is proposed or begun. There are no exceptions to this: not one, not ever. The reason is simple. If there were no forces or beliefs in contradiction of the proposals or change the change would have happened already. Either people tend to believe in what they are doing or they have become comfortable and change is not received with open arms. If everyone agreed with every change, there would be no consistency and sanity in the world. So, you now see that resistance to change is not only normal, but good. Remember, then, through any attempt to bring about change, look for resistance and include plans for overcoming resistance in everything you do. Often it can be helpful to engage a consultant to help identify resistance and to create a plan for responding. A consultant can be perceived as more objective and can also say some things very directly and then leave town!

Internal

The reason schools often find that after ten years of "successful coeducation" there are still some problems is because they have done a good job of anticipating and ameliorating the external constraints, but have tended to miss or ignore the more difficult internal ones.

Given the previous definition of external constraint, the term internal constraint refers to the internal state of the person(s) being constrained. The gender research identifies self-esteem as the most powerful of the internal constraints. Additional constraints could be such things as ability or talent, training or knowledge, mental or emotional health. Examples:

1) After the algebra II level, only 20 percent of girls take additional math while 80 percent of boys take additional math. The internal constraint may be that girls believe they are not capable in math and cannot compete with boys.

2) The coeducational cheerleading squad has never had a male member. The internal constraint may be that the boys are afraid of being labeled as "sissies."

The logical action would be to remove or reduce the internal constraints. We have just arrived at the wall! Unfortunately, logic alone cannot help generate effective actions for internal restraints. This is true for several reasons. First, identification of the cause of the imbalance is very complicated. Second, internal constraints are very resistant to change. If, for example, a girl does not go on to calculus because she experiences severe math anxiety, strategies for overcoming math anxiety often take a long-term commitment, can require professional help, and have no guarantee of success. And, finally, there is very little agreement in the professional world about how to mold belief systems so that what girls have traditionally done is perceived as positive and appropriate for boys, or vice versa.

Yes, dealing with internal constraints is difficult, but not impossible. Here are some suggestions for action for the above:

1) Beginning with algebra I, create an all-girls section and employ recommended methods for teaching math to girls.

Single-gender classes have the reported effect of gradually increasing the self-esteem of girls and their beliefs that they can do math.

2) Have a day when the cheerleaders work with the weight-lifting class to develop a team cheer that requires great strength. Continue pairing the cheerleaders with various male groups in the school until it becomes ordinary to see males and females doing cheers together. Remember the Anna Quindlen story?

Most situations, when analyzed have some inequity and there are usually both internal and external constraints operating. It means that it takes longer to do the analysis and requires great thought, creativity, flexibility, and courage to identify and to put effective actions into place.

Let's consider a worst case scenario:

A boys' school has recently turned coeducational. There are four boys for every girl, the faculty is 70 percent male and the administration is 100 percent male. Female applicants report that the atmosphere does not feel "comfortable" when they visit the school and only 25 percent of female visitors actually apply to the school.

All of this data would have been evident after completing a numerical assessment and doing follow-up data collection related to possible causality. The recommended action is to equalize opportunities, remove external constraints, and remove or reduce internal constraints.

Here goes!

a) Hire a consultant.

b) Design the admission visits differently for female applicants. For example, have a present female student call her the night before her visit and give her some options of classes to visit, answer questions for her, etc.

c) Alter the visual impact of the school. For example, move the hundreds of pictures of male alumni from the front hall to the alumni room.

d) Make sure all of the school's literature has female pictures, etc.

e) Add a female to the administration, even if it means having the female athletic director join the administration.

f) Contact area universities and offer to provide field placements, internships, or student teaching opportunities for their female students.

g) Invite the area girls' school to participate in theater and social events (Good luck — they'll think you're trying to steal their girls!).

By now you can see which of the above suggestions deal with numerical inequity, external constraints, internal constraints, or any combination of these. The above list could continue for several pages. As you think about it, it is really necessary to have two concurrent plans. First, put into place some fairly easy and inexpensive actions that can alleviate some or one of the issues. If possible, this should be a high visibility, low cost, and popular action. This is the short-term plan (which usually deals with external constraints). It also serves the purpose of getting people on board and interested in the next steps. At the same time that you are planning short-term actions, time needs to be spent making a long-term plan. A long-term plan often gets to the causes of issues and works over a period of time to remove or to alter those causes (which often include those change-resistant internal constraints). A good example of this is a school where far fewer girls than boys take advanced placement math. There are usually many root causes, such as girls who have developed math anxiety or have a low view of their capability, teachers who have not been trained to work with math-anxious or math-challenged girls, a curriculum that is not female friendly, parents who do not do those things that encourage girls to take math, etc. The long-term plan would include teacher training, parent education, curriculum analysis, possible single-gender math classes or math support systems for girls, as well as many other possible actions.

It is better to put into action one change that can ameliorate several problems at once. Because of the natural system's resistance, it is easier to get one thing accepted rather than a barrage of changes. Strategies to look for are ones with a multiplicative impact, that is ones that have a short-term and long-term impact, and that can deal with internal and external constraints. It is the synergy of the two parallel strategies — those that deal with external constraints and those that deal with internal constraints when combined in an educational system that yield the most powerful effects. Some examples are:

■ Single-gender classes — powerful short-term results (happier, satisfied students) and significant long-term results (better grades, test scores, and higher percentage of students going on to advanced placement courses)

■ Mentoring/Modeling — same results as above

■ Strengthening self-esteem — see chapter three

■ Serious and comprehensive teacher training with follow-up video analysis of teachers — not just one gender awareness workshop, but ongoing training in techniques and application, and review of teaching. Videotaping doesn't have to be threatening. It can be done by each teacher and viewed with a trusted colleague.

■ Direct teaching of gender issues to students — this is very difficult (the affective education movement has been a dismal failure), but not impossible. For instance, you might explain to high school girls and boys about the vagus nerve in the face. Since the part of the brain that is related to the sensation of touch is much larger in females than males, females prefer a light touch to their face, or a gentle kiss. Boys who have learned about this have altered their kissing behavior. This can be the beginning of a meaningful coeducational conversation that will lead to real understanding, appreciation, and acceptance of gender differences (and similarities).

It is critical that schools educate themselves about all these issues if they are serious about gender equity in the classroom and the school community. Schools should consider both the external and internal barriers to gender equity.

But all this leads us to the next chapter, which focuses solely on the self-esteem of girls. With the increase in anecdotal research, clarity about internal factors correlated with observed behavior suggests quite clearly that females have decreasing self-esteem and that this deteriorating internal factor negatively influences behavior and decision making in females in a big way. For females, negative self-esteem is very pervasive. If the self-esteem of girls could be improved, this would have a positive impact on beliefs and behavior. In other words, in the examples given above, girls may feel strong and capable enough to speak out in class or to take that advanced placement physics course, regardless of the climate of the classroom or the pedagogical techniques of the teacher.

The self-esteem factor, then, is key to the successful realization of gender equity. Girls with low self-esteem can, and probably will, sabotage even the best laid plans and programs for equitable gender opportunities. Even if a teacher uses such methods as "wait time" to help equalize student input by gender, if the girls in the class do not believe in their capability, they still will not increase their oral input. The key to leveling the gender playing field is a synergistic combination of dealing with the inequitable external constraints while also taking dead aim at the most serious internal constraint: self-esteem in girls. This must be done (and it cannot be stressed strongly enough) in a premeditated way over time.

CHAPTER THREE

SELF-ESTEEM IS GREEN

"If you think you can, you can.
And if you think you can't, you're right."

— *Mary Kay Ash*

Almost all writings about self-esteem or self-concept start with the question: What do these words mean? Everyone seems to know, yet the ambiguity of the definitions makes the analysis of problems related to self-esteem quite difficult. One of the best (and shortest) discussions of this problem is contained in the first few pages of *Building Self, Adolescent Girls and Self-Esteem* by Sundra Flansburg (1993). It is an excellent summary of the concept of self-esteem; please read it!

While you've got your reading glasses perched on your nose, please check out the "Self-Esteem" resources at the end of this chapter.

You may have noticed the more frequent use of the term "self-esteem" over "self-concept" in the above sources. There is good reason for this. Self-esteem implies confidence and satisfaction in oneself, or one's good opinion of oneself. Self-concept, on the other hand, is more neutral, implying something conceived in the mind, a thought or an idea of oneself. Thus, self-esteem is the term that fits best. When you think about it, everyone has a thought or idea of herself/himself. That may include that I think I am a tomato! Since our stated focus is the internal state that is inextricably tied to emotion and behavior, a valence, an evaluative component, seems to be needed. Ergo, whether I think I am a good tomato or a bad tomato is more to the point. Therefore, self-esteem is the preferred terminology, since this term includes an evaluative opinion of one-self.

Terminology decision made, the next step is to be as specific as possible about the components of self-esteem. If a degree of specificity can be reached, there is hope for developing strategies to facilitate the development of self-esteem in all students, especially in the population deemed at risk in this area: females.

Everyone who ever wrote about, studied, or researched self-esteem has listed two to five components that blend together to create this internal state. Many of these components overlap, some do not. There is some agreement about them, there is more dis-agreement. In this case we must ask ourselves one question: What are the components or characteristics or things that, if they were not present, would make it impossible to have self-esteem?

At a recent education conference, one teacher suggested that beauty was a component of self-esteem. She must have forgotten about Marilyn Monroe! Certainly feeling positive about your body would be a nice addition, but the litmus test is that you can't have self-esteem without it. Holding characteristics to this light, Porsches, good health, a loving mother, all fall by the wayside. Again, these would be nice additions, but in their absence, many people have very high levels of self-esteem. So, what are these elusive compo-nents? At the last three conferences at which I spoke, I presented three components for the audience to consider. So far, no one has argued against these three as passing the litmus test. There have been arguments for additions, but none for the deletion of one of the big three. That's a very good start. If we can agree on three components, we should be able to combine this with what we know about girls and then develop school structures, programs, and opportunities to enhance self-esteem.

Drum roll, please! The three requisite components of self-esteem are:

Green Frogs
Green Fingernails
Green Marbles

Well, my school's color is green and I needed to tell stories to the students so that the components of self-esteem would become meaningful to them. It also seems to be true that adults enjoy and remember stories that are meaningful. Could this have been the catalyst for the first fable?

Green Frogs

Once upon a time there was a little girl named JoAnn. Every summer she and her family would spend several weeks at a fishing camp in the Canadian wilderness, complete with outhouses and black flies. The summer of her fifth birthday seemed like each summer before it: drive forever, sit in the back seat and get sick, wake up late at night and board a boat to be transported across the lake to the fishing camp.

All was as expected the next morning. The camp was filled — mostly with men and a few families. All of the children were boys, except JoAnn. She was also the youngest child in the camp again that year. Oh well, she jumped into the boat with her lunch and her family (mom, dad, eight-year-old brother) for a full day of fishing.

Later that day, as the sun began to set, all of the fishermen, one fisher woman (JoAnn's mother), and one fisher girl (JoAnn), returned to camp. Although everyone was usually ravenous and wanted to head to the main lodge and the dining room, the tradition was that the fish had to be cleaned, a hole dug in the deep sawdust of the barn, and the fish laid up against the huge blocks of ice under the sawdust. The blocks of ice had been cut from the lake in the winter and lasted all summer under the protection of the mountain of sawdust. Every family marked where they had buried their fish with a big stick. Part of the fun was deciding what to put on the stick for identification. JoAnn's family usually chose one of Marty's (JoAnn's brother) socks, since they were quite distinctive with embroidered diamond designs on the ankles.

But on this first night of fishing camp, no one had any fish, except one man. This was quite strange since Healy Lake was famous for its abundance of fish and everyone caught their limit every day. Discussion at dinner that night in the lodge was quite animated. Everyone gathered around the successful fisherman to find out his secret. It didn't take long before it was discovered that he had only used frogs as bait, no worms, no lures, only frogs.

As the adults were sitting around and drinking cold Canadian beer (also stored up against the ice, next to the fish in the barn), the children, as usual, got together to play. But instead of playing, they decided to get into the serious business of price fixing. You see, the plan was to get up very early the next morning and go frog catching. All agreed that five cents a frog was fair.

Frogs like to hunker down in the tall grass right next to the lake. So, where to go frog hunting the next morning was no mystery. The children fanned out and established their own frog territory and spent the next half hour in serious pursuit of their amphibious victims. Everyone caught some, pretty much in direct correlation with their age. Just as planned, the froggers headed up to the dock, where the fishermen and fisher woman were getting their boats ready for the day. Frogs were in great demand and every frogger was sold out of his/her stock within minutes. Marty made a whopping quarter, JoAnn was happy with her dime. After all, she had smaller hands and was not quite as dexterous as the older boys.

That night, everyone eagerly headed to the big rock where the fish were cleaned. There were more fish tonight, but the number of fish caught seemed to be exactly analogous to the number of frogs that each fisherman, fisher woman, or fisher girl had used. And, another startling discovery was made! All of the very large bass or pike that were caught were not caught with just any old frog — they were caught with a "greenie!" The children shivered, because they instinctively knew that the price of a "greenie" (they get their name from being totally green) would be much higher than just any old regular frog. The problem was that "greenies" are very hard to catch. They have no brown on them like ordinary old frogs and are harder to see. Also, they're very skinny, very quick, and seem to have eyes in the back of their heads (since they always see a hand that is about to ensnare them).

No child slept much that night, dreaming of the possible wealth of the next day. Because, before departing to their individual cabins for the night, the children again engaged in P.F. (price fixing, that is). A "greenie" would cost a quarter tomorrow!

The sun was barely up before the froggers were out skirting the edge of the lake. No one was talking much; the belief was that "greenies" could hear anything. Time went by quickly, because that's what happens when you're chasing "greenies." Just before the boats were ready to depart, the children came running to the dock with their treasures. Everyone, except JoAnn, caught one greenie, and the oldest boy had two. JoAnn knew it was because she was too young to be fast enough to capture a "greenie," but she still felt awful as everyone "set sail" for a long day of fishing.

Dusk arrived, boats returned, fishermen, fisher woman, and fisher girl all headed to the big rock. Things hadn't changed. This was weird. The fish would bite only on frogs, nothing else, and the "greenies" had been the bait again for the largest fish.

Well, it doesn't take a genius to know that the next day's "greenie" market value was going to be fifty cents! If you're already beginning to feel sorry for JoAnn, don't! She had spent some of her time the last two mornings not only watching the other froggers, but especially watching the frogs — the green ones. She was convinced that she would be able to catch many "greenies" the next day. So, before she went to bed, she asked her dad how much six "fifty-centses" would be.

Dawn arrived. Froggers tore out of their cabins and headed to the tall grass by the lake. Fishermen and fisher woman began packing the days necessities in their boats, and soon it was time to leave. The froggers arrived at the docks, breathless. It was a bad frogging morning, only two "greenies" amongst all of the froggers, but a lot of those old ordinary brown frogs. And then, JoAnn pushed her way to the front. To everyone's fall-flat-on-your-face astonishment, she had six "greenies" in her small bucket and none of those old ordinary brown frogs. JoAnn had a hard time sleeping that night. She said her cheeks hurt from smiling so much all day!

There is a strategy that is effective to this day for catching green frogs. If you buy this book and write to me, I'll tell you, since this is a true story and the names have not been changed to protect the *competent.*

Competence — the first of the three ingredients needed for self-esteem.

Green Fingernails

Since 1896, student volunteering had always been a part of our school's history. Lately, interest had waned and the administration was seeking ways of revitalizing this important connection with the larger community. The head of school had heard about the well-known volunteer program at a girls' school in the east and decided to send the two faculty advisors of our emaciated program to visit this school. Off to the east went the school psychologist and the French teacher, both passionate about bringing back the spark that would ignite the students volunteering passions. Little did they know that what they would bring back, in addition to that spark, was the knowledge of one of the components of self-esteem!

Denise and JoAnn, the two passionate advisors of the volunteer program, arrived on the campus two days early and found they had time to explore other facets of the school. Denise headed for the French classes. JoAnn headed for the screams. Can you tell who was the French teacher and who was the psychologist?

The screams seemed to be coming from a tall collection of rocks that an Ohioan would call a small mountain, however these girls called it many other names, most of which could not be printed. The absolute focal point of the screams was easy to ascertain upon arrival at the bottom of the mini-cliff. It was coming from the mouth of a very petite blonde girl, very nicely dressed, hair fashionably styled, fingernails polished ever so perfectly. She was standing on the top of a rock about seven feet from the ground with a rope tied around her middle. This rope extended to the top of the cliff where a faculty advisor was leaning over the edge saying words of encouragement to the girl below.

The look on JoAnn's face must have caused a nearby adult to come over and offer an explanation. "You see," she said, "these are the freshmen and this is their on-campus challenge course. All ninth graders participate in these activities for the first semester of school while the sophomores, juniors, and seniors go into the city for their weekly volunteer jobs." She went on to say that these experiences were part of the orientation program and served many purposes. Her discourse was cut off by a much louder, longer penetrating scream.

As JoAnn's attention returned to the cliff, the cause of the scream was clear. The girl had moved up the cliff to about ten feet and was sharing her fear and frustration with her advisor at the top. She begged to be let down or pulled up by the rope, explained convincingly that her muscles were giving out and she was about to faint. Her final wail: "I can't do it." From up above came the response: "Yes, you can!" You could almost see the girl calculating what it would take to get someone to rescue her. Then... she let go of the rock.

Well, the previous screams were nothing compared to this one! It must really hurt to have a rope cinched tightly around your waist holding your entire body weight. Have you noticed, in times of crisis, some people notice strange details? Just then JoAnn saw the girl's fingernails — they were very long and nicely shaped, and painted green! She was so focused on her fingernails that the observer almost missed the look that flashed across the girl's face. Surprisingly, it seemed to be one of anger.

In the next instant the girl reached out, grabbed the nearest rock and regained her purchase. The cost was one broken, green fingernail. She climbed another several feet, another broken fingernail. At that point she looked up and seemed to be about to say something, but looked at her advisor's face and continued to climb. We, the audience at the bottom of the cliff and the audience at the top of the cliff (advisor and other students), were mesmerized by the display in front of us. She was sweating now, her hair was not so neat, and she was breaking a green fingernail at the rate of one per every three or four vertical feet. But it was her face that was most riveting. The previous looks of fear and frustration had faded. The closer she got to the top, the more frequently she looked at her advisor. The ground audience was in agreement — her advisor should run for cover before she got to the top!

Well, she did get to the top, sans green fingernails. Faces can be so expressive. No one will ever forget hers as she gained her footing on the top of the cliff. She looked as if she could climb a real mountain, like one of those in Nepal. She then turned on her heel, headed directly to her advisor and the hug was very long and sincere.

The girl's name? I never found out, or she would receive a copy of this book for providing such a great story for the second component of self-esteem — **confidence**.

Green Marbles

Perhaps it was the eels swimming in the small pool in the living room that made them unforgettable. Who really knows? But as we scooped out the eels to save them for dinner later and began to drain the pool, that's when it happened. Marty fell in love. Falling in love is not a strange occurrence usually, but in this case, it bordered on being strange. You see, the object, or objects (to be more precise) of Marty's lustful gaze were very large green marbles. These green marbles lined the bottom of the pool and were responsible for the dazzling green color of the water. Now, the time had come to remove the marbles. My friend Don was moving and my nephew Marty and I were there to help. Marty was six at the time.

Four years later and several inches taller, Marty came running into the house with a look on his face that was filled with concern. "Aunt JoAnn!" My breathing stopped until his next words tumbled out, "I forgot Carey's birthday party is tonight and I have nothing to take and it starts at 7:00 and..." I didn't even let him finish. Super Aunt to the rescue! "Don't worry, Marty, I just got paid, we can swing by the mall, buy a present and have it wrapped and be at Carey's house..." It was his turn not to let me finish. I will never forget that look on his face. Now, twenty years later, I realize that look said, "I love you, but you are too dumb to live, but I'll tell you that gently." "But Aunt JoAnn," the wise ten year old said, "It won't mean anything."

Marty disappeared into the jungle known as his bedroom and reappeared with a large bucket of green marbles. Yes, Don had given them to him right after he was brave enough to take a bite of eel. Those marbles occupied a sacred place by the head of Marty's bed. That way, he could see them before he fell asleep and as soon as he awakened. Love is like that.

"Marty, you love those marbles! Why don't we take half of them and put them in a nice box for Carey?" The same look appeared on his face and I knew what he was going to say: "But, Aunt JoAnn, it won't mean anything." I remembered then that his cousin Carey held a special place in Marty's heart. She was just that kind of person, but she was also eight years old! We were about to head to a party where Marty was the only boy and a house full of eight-year-old girls would be oohing and aahing over Carey's presents as she opened them.

We were halfway there and I knew I had made a mistake. I should have called Carey's mother and warned her that the somewhat unclean bucket of green marbles was not really green marbles at all, but a bucket of Marty's love. With her prompting, Carey would ooh and aah over this present along with all of the others. But it was too late.

The car stopped, Marty grabbed the bucket of marbles and sprinted into the house. By the time I entered, the gift-wrapped bucket of marbles sat in the midst of the table of presents. My worst fears were confirmed. Carey sat in the middle of a horde of girls opening presents. A Barbie doll, barrettes, games and toys were all unwrapped. It was obvious, she was saving Marty's present for the very last.

It was time. She reached for the large bundle, but could not move it. The other girls helped push it over to her end of the table. I looked at Marty — his eyes were shining with excitement and pride. With a huge smile on her face, Carey ripped open the paper... and the smile promptly disappeared. It seemed like forever before she looked up from the green marbles. With tears in her eyes, she looked at Marty, her voice filled with emotion, and said, "This is the best present I've ever had." I knew then why this girl was so beloved.

He floated to the car. The next day he tried out for little league baseball and did not make the team. "Oh well, I guess I'll try soccer."

The aftermath of green marble giving was pretty powerful!

Connectedness— the third component of self-esteem. It really refers to the opposite of what many purported self-esteem programs profess. Self, analysis of self, appreciation of self are often the core of affective education programs. However, the evidence is quite clear; these programs are not very effective affective programs. Focusing on self does not increase self-esteem, but it can increase selfishness. Connecting with another human being, feeling a part of a group or community, giving, caring, are all examples of connectedness. It is by focusing outward rather than inward that self is enhanced. God has an incredible sense of humor!

Competence, confidence, and connectedness are the three critical components of self-esteem. If any one of the three is absent, it is impossible for self-esteem to be high. If schools provide opportunities for children to experience these components, the most insidious internal constraint will be diminished. Just think, if we could improve the self-esteem of girls there may not be a gender discrepancy in advanced placement courses, the "air" studies would show equity, and more girls would become professional froggers — or, perhaps, engineers.

The above three C's can't be taught or improved by discussion or self analysis; they must be experienced. The key is to provide the experiences or opportunities that will allow the individual to experience each C "enough" to enhance self-esteem. If situations are very dramatic, one experience can be very powerful and sometimes change a person forever. More often, experiences need to be layered over time.

Another important point to think about is the balance and synergy of the three C's as critical to self-esteem. All three need to be present and somewhat equal to yield the highest level of self-esteem. For example, the person who has a high level of connectedness but much lower levels of confidence and competence will be less likely to take risks or to face conflict than if there were high levels of all C ingredients. This provides a very critical diagnostic measure of self-esteem as well as a guide to deciding strategies for self-esteem enhancement. That is, if a person is low in competence, strategies or programs need to be made available that will develop this person's competence in a meaningful area. One clear example of this is math anxiety in girls. The strategy is not to make them feel better about their perceived inability, but to increase their performance capability. Teach them how to do math!

This may be a good place to explain why math examples and concerns are a central focus of this book. Consider these points:

- Colleges are influenced greatly by applicants who take and do well in advanced placement math courses or tests. Ergo, admission to college is impacted significantly.

- Most predictions of employment opportunities for the future indicate that our technologically based world will require extensive background and knowledge in math.

- The AAUW study (*Shortchanging Girls, Shortchanging America*) showed a significant correlation between a female's self-esteem and her perception of her mathematical skills. This correlation did not exist with any other subject area.

- It is important that girls are offered a strong educational program in all academic areas — and that their individual strengths and interests are encouraged. At this point in time, however, it is essential for girls to do as much math as possible.

For the sake of efficiency and effectiveness, it makes sense that those opportunities or programs which affect all three C's would be the most powerful and yield the most significant impact. Let's take a look at four educational programs that are fairly popular as a result of the recent gender research. All of these programs have the potential to increase all three C's. Unfortunately many are not structured or planned adequately enough to realize this power and the outcome is left to serendipity.

Mentoring

Connectedness — By their very nature, mentoring programs provide opportunities for their participants to experience connectedness — being a meaningful part of something or someone other than self. The problem with many mentoring programs is that they are too short-term or "one shot" opportunities and therefore do not allow the connectedness to develop fully. Programs that extend over a year or more tend to have more long lasting effects on connectedness and, subsequently, self-esteem. The dorm programs for female math majors at several universities are an example of this. Other good examples are programs that connect girls with professionals in fields of interest to the girls. If a middle school girl wants to be an artist, for example, she is connected with an adult artist in the community and the two of them have the opportunity to interact together many times over a several year period.

Competence — This component is not necessarily a part of many mentoring programs and needs to be deliberately planned and inserted. In one public school in Warren, Ohio, computer experts from a local business come into the school over a year's period and teach their "mentees" (all elementary students) how to use the computers that their company has donated to the school.

Confidence — Although this can be the by-product of experiences that lead to competence, it cannot be taken for granted that this will happen. It needs to be a planned part of the mentoring experience. To take the above example, mentors could train their mentees in using a software program, to memorize math facts, and to work with them until this is an automatic skill and they get an A on a timed math fact quiz. Confidence is something that almost magically forms from connectedness, competence, and doing or using the newly formed competence.

Challenge Courses (Outward Bound-type experiences)

Connectedness — A group that works together over a period of time to overcome a common obstacle connects. It is as simple and as complex as that. Whether you have filled sand bags to save your hometown from a flood, or just lived through a rope's course together, it works. There is some validity to the statement that the more serious, difficult, or dangerous the task, the deeper the connectedness.

Competence — Because of its very nature, challenge courses provide the opportunity to build competence. Learning from each other, failing and trying again, developing strategies that work are all part of this.

Confidence — Please reread the green fingernail story; there is no need to say more here.

Many challenge courses are individually based. These work particularly well if the person involved is low in competence or confidence. If connectedness is also an issue, individual challenge courses obviously do nothing to improve this. For institutions, trying to achieve the highest gain for the most people for the least cost means that group challenge courses are more effective than individual courses. For those individuals who are not athletically or physically talented, there are challenge courses that rely on thinking skills and group interdependence that accomplish the same goals.

Cooperative Learning

Connectedness — Although it is often assumed that cooperative learning techniques fulfill the requisite for connectedness, which is why they are recommended for girls, this is not necessarily the case. The experiences need to be structured in such a way that the participants of the group will interact in a positive way and the structure of the task is such that everyone will participate. This is no easy feat! A class that is told to form groups of four and find the answer to a physics problem or to discuss the role of a character in a novel often fail to achieve connectedness. The group needs to be balanced to promote interaction — not too many leaders or too many followers. Therefore, given the literature indicating the possible dominance of boys in a coeducational setting, the balance of gender in the formation of cooperative groups needs to be a consideration, too. The sources for cooperative learning in the bibliography give helpful examples of how to form effective groups.

Competence — The same is true for this component. Learning tasks need to be structured so that the members of the group will become more competent because of working together. This often means putting a diverse group of learners/performers together so that the strong suit of each learner combines to create a powerful group effect.

Confidence — If the above two C's are realized, the probability of the group members becoming more confident is greatly increased, but not always. Continuing work with the same group, repetitive experiences, rehearsals, etc. all work together to increase the confidence of the group and need to be imbedded in the cooperative learning experience. Group confidence, over time, generalizes to individual confidence.

Effective cooperative learning experiences for all members of the group are extremely difficult to achieve, which is why many teachers try, but do not continue with, this approach. It requires knowledge of how to form effective groups, how to define tasks that require the participation of every student in each group, and how to carefully monitor the work of the groups. But don't give up; with some additional reading and experimentation, most teachers report powerful changes in attitude and production of students in a cooperative learning environment.

Single-Gender Classes

Connectedness — The research suggests that, with boys removed, females in class become more interactive and comfortable. This experience over time leads to a sense of connectedness within the group, through helping one another, listening to, and accepting each others points of view, etc.

Competence — This component often follows in an all-female class because of the sense of comfort and willingness to take risks.

In addition, changing pedagogical techniques to better fit females can ensure the increase in competence of the girls in a class.

Confidence — From the literature, this seems to be the most common and immediate effect of single-gender classes. Girls report that they are more confident about talking in class, tackling problems, and expressing their ideas. Therefore, it does not seem to be necessary to plan for the development of confidence, but merely to provide the opportunity of a single-gender educational experience.

The above four programs are the Big Four; they have shown the most significant impact on the self-esteem and subsequent behavior and performance of the girls. Many other singular strategies are available and important in the overall planning of strategies and programs for gender equity. It really is a matter of taking the time and effort required to analyze a system thoroughly, to make a comprehensive plan to develop equitable programs which will remove or reduce both external and internal constraints, and to put those plans into effect.

Resources

Cooperative Learning:

Brandt, Ronald S. *Cooperative Learning And The Collaborative School.* Alexandria, Virginia: Association for Supervision and Curriculum Development. 1991.

Heredia-Arriaga, Sue and Dr. Duane Campbell. *Integrating Cooperative Learning: An Introduction for the Elementary Classroom Teacher.* Video and teacher resource guide. Carson City, Nevada: Superior Learning Programs. 1996.

The Cooperative Learning Catalog. California: Kagan Cooperative Learning. Published yearly.

Johnson, David W. *Cooperative Learning in the Classroom.* Alexandria, Virginia: Association for Supervision and Curriculum Development. 1994.

Walker, Dot and Pamela Brown. *Pathways To Co-Operation: Starting Points For Cooperative Learning.* Australia: Eleanor Curtain Publishing, Inc. 1994.

Mentoring/Modeling:

Bird, Stephanie. *Mentoring Means Future Scientists: A Guide to Developing Mentoring Programs Based on the AWIS Mentoring Project.* Washington, D.C.: Association for Women in Science, 1993.

Faddis, Bonnie et al. *Hand in Hand: Mentoring Young Women: Guide for Planning, Implementing, and Evaluating a Mentoring Program. Hand in Hand: Mentoring Young Women: Ideabook for Mentors. Hand in Hand: Mentoring Young Women: Student Career Journal.* Massachusetts: WEEA Publishing Center, Education Development Center, Inc., 1988.

Fort, Deborah C., ed. *A Hand Up: Women Mentoring Women in Science.* Washington, D.C.: The Association for Women in Science, 1995.

Gurian, Michael. *The Wonder of Boys: What Parents, Mentors, and Educators Can Do to Shape Boys into Exceptional Men.* New York: G.P. Putnam's Sons, 1996.

Hanson, Elizabeth. "Reaching Out to Gifted Girls Through Television: Studying Television Role Models." *Gifted Child Today.* May/June 1995.

Mobley, Gloria. "Internships for Girls." *Education Week,* October 12, 1994.

Saito, Rebecca N. and Dale A. Blyth. "Mentoring Relationships Benefit Adults and Students." *School Team Innovator.* December 1994/January 1995.

Self-Esteem:

Akin, Terri, et al. *The Best Self-Esteem Activities: For the Elementary Grades.* California: Innerchoice Publishing, 1990.

Allard, Andrea and Jeni Wilson. *Gender Dimensions: Developing Interpersonal Skills in the Classroom.* Australia: Eleanor Curtain Publishing, 1995.

Begun, Ruth Weltmann, ed. *Ready to Use: Social Skills Lessons and Activities for Grades 4-6.* New York: The Center for Applied Research in Education, 1996.

Bingham, Mindy and Sandy Stryker. *Things Will Be Different for My Daughter: A Practical Guide to Building Her Self-Esteem and Self-Reliance.* New York: Penguin Books, 1995.

Blais, Madeleine. *In These Girls, Hope Is a Muscle.* New York: The Atlantic Monthly Press, 1995.

Borba, Michele. *Esteem Builders: A K-8 Self-Esteem Curriculum for Improving Student Achievement: Behavior and School Climate.* Torrance, California: Jalamar Press, 1989.

Canfield, Jack and Harold Clive Wells. *100 Ways to Enhance Self-Concept in the Classroom.* Massachusetts: Allyn and Bacon, 1994.

Flansburg, Sundra. *Center for Equity and Cultural Diversity Working Paper Two: Building Self: Adolescent Girls and Self-Esteem.* Massachusetts: WEEA Publishing Center, Educational Development Center, Inc., 1993.

Gilligan, Carol. *In a Different Voice.* Cambridge, Massachusetts: Harvard University Press, 1982.

Katz, Lilian G. and Diane E. McClellan. *The Teacher's Role in the Social Development of Young Children.* Illinois: ERIC Clearinghouse on Elementary and Early Childhood Education, University of Illinois, 1991.

Kenway, Jane and Sue Willis. *Hearts and Minds; Self-Esteem and the Schooling of Girls.* New York: The Falmer Press, 1990.

Pipher, Mary. *Reviving Ophelia: Saving the Selves of Adolescent Girls.* New York: G.P. Putman's Sons, 1994.

Promoting Self-Esteem in Young Women: A Manual for Teachers. New York: The University of New York and the State Education Department Division of Civil Rights and Intercultural Relations, 1989.

"The Confidence Quotient: Building Girls' Self-Esteem." *Keeping the Trust, A Quarterly Report from the Cleveland Foundation,* Summer, 1992.

Wade, Rahima Carol. *Joining Hands: From Personal to Planetary Friendship in the Primary Classroom.* Arizona: Zephyr Press, 1991.

Single-Gender Education:

Hollinger, Debra and Rebecca Adamson, eds. "Single-Sex Schooling: Proponents Speak." *Vol. II, A Special Report from the Office of Educational Research and Improvement,* U.S. Department of Education, 1992.

"Issues Involving Single-Gender Schools and Programs." *A Report to the Chairman,* Committee on the Budget, House of Representatives, May 1996.

Lawton, Millicent. "Bias Against Girls Found in Both Coed, One-Sex Schools." *Education Week,* June 10, 1992.

Riordan, Cornelius. *Girls and Boys in School: Together or Separate?* New York: Teachers College, Columbia University, 1990.

Sedgwick, John. "What Difference Does a Single-Sex School Make to a Girl Later in Life?" *Self Magazine.* March 1997.

"Single-Sex Schooling: Perspectives from Practice and Research." *Vol. I, A Special Report from the Office of Educational Research and Improvement.* U.S. Department of Education, 1992.

"Boys and Girls/ Together and Apart." *Independent School,* Fall 1992.

CHAPTER FOUR

CRUCIBLE MOMENTS, CRUCIBLE EVENTS

"Never mistake knowledge for wisdom.
One helps you make a living; one helps you make a life."

— *Sandra Carey*

We know that gender inequities exist. We know that schools need to look carefully at their own programs to uncover (and remove) the barriers to equitable education. We know that self-esteem is the key to success in school. We know what programs help build self-esteem in girls. So what's left?

The experience of everyday life.

The question for this chapter is: What is important for educators (teachers, administrators, *and* parents) to think about and to do during the formative years to help foster the development of healthy and strong girls? What advice is succinct yet specific enough, wise yet practical enough, simple enough to put into practice, but complex enough to have a lasting effect?

Succinct and simple come first. One of the best ways to illustrate this is with the strudel theory. Strudel? Yes, strudel. Creating a strudel is very much like putting together, over time, the recipe and ingredients for the development of a healthy and strong child. All of us are the accumulation of genetic material intricately combined with the impact of environmental experiences layered over time — like filo dough in a strudel. Basic strudel theory says that the critical core of educating and parenting is to think premeditatedly and carefully and to plan those experiences, in small increments, that over days and weeks and months and years help layer and therefore build the inner core of a child.

Do I really mean that every little experience, every second of being and of responding to a child as a parent or a teacher is critical? Well, yes, to a degree. However, the good news is that children, who basically feel loved and are part of an environment that feels relatively safe and consistent, can withstand many parental mistakes and teachable moments not handled particularly well by well intentioned adults. Although parenting is often serendipitous and reactive to things like how much sleep your daughter had the night before and therefore her level of crankiness the next day, that is not the substance of this chapter. It is our response to the crucible events or moments that I want to focus on. It is critical for all of us to have thought about in terms of child development and how our responses can be part of layering the strudel in positive ways. If we do it wrong, we can impede the development of self-esteem.

How crucible moments/events are handled is critical because these life experiences have the potential of not only having a layering effect on development that cannot be easily undone, but they can also have a dramatic and significant immediate effect that can be deeply imbedded in the system. As professed in chapter three, we need to teach girls how to catch green frogs and not to care if (periodically) they break a fingernail freshly painted with beautiful green nail polish. We need to know how important it is to give a beloved bucket of green marbles to someone else. Premeditatedly arranging the *doing* of these experiences over time is critical to the long-term development of the self-esteem of children. But life also happens to us, regardless of our planning. So, in addition to layering the doing of such things in the lives of children, we need to think how we should react when these life events occur.

To clarify, there are crucible moments and there are crucible events. The former often catch us in a reactive mode, without much time for thought. The latter, crucible events are/will be present in everyone's life to some extent, so we can proactively think through the core concepts that are critical for the healthy development of a child. I use the word "crucible" because it clearly captures the significance to the forging of the individual who is in the experiencing seat of these moments or events.

Some of the most critical of the crucible events in the seemingly never-ending formative years of most humans include those around:

1) discipline

2) risk-taking

3) change

4) loss/separation

5) friendship

A picture may be worth a thousand words, but in terms of understanding human beings, a story must be worth a million! Lois's story captures the essence of the issues related to crucible event #1 — discipline:

Lois was sent to my office because she had defaced school property, which in this case meant that she had written a negative statement on the classroom wall about her second-grade homeroom teacher. No one had seen her do this, but it happened right after Lois was not chosen to speak during any of the reading class time (and talking to an audience was one of her most cherished experiences). Everyone could tell that Lois was not happy. Also, handwriting analysis of the wall missive did not require the skill of an expert to recognize the distinctive penmanship that was Lois's.

For reasons that can only be speculative at this time, Lois seemed to have experienced discipline as synonymous with punishment. So, when Lois walked into my office, she had "the look": "I'm innocent and I will lie through my teeth to prove it to you." She was braced and ready for the onslaught.

But discipline is not synonymous with punishment according to the strudel theory of human development and this was a crucible moment. Lois sat down and composed her face into the pained innocent-about-to-be-accused look. "Lois," I said, "do you remember when you got in a fight on the playground when you were in kindergarten and you explained to me that you hit a person because she had done something bad to someone else? You were so upset about what you considered the bad behavior of the other girl, that you didn't care about breaking the school rule and you told the truth about hitting, even though you knew you would get into trouble for doing that. Then, I remember the time when you came to tell me that you didn't think it was fair that only new students were given Laurel buckets when they came to school for new student orientation, and their assigned buddies, who were to take them around the school on that day, didn't get one. Again, I was impressed that you had the courage to tell me that you thought I was doing something that wasn't fair, even though I am the director here. I've always admired you because you try to be honest even when it is scary for you. Now you're here, and you're scared because you know I have to punish the person who wrote something unkind on the wall about Mrs. Carr."

To make a very long story much shorter, this strategy of acknowledging Lois's basic nature, of setting the tone that she is respected and that this would not only be about punishment seemed to be helpful, but not sufficient. She lied and denied that her hand and her writing instrument had been instrumental in the finished product on the wall. So, I had to add the clean-state part: I had a terrible memory, I told her, and after we had settled this episode, in the future when I saw her, none of this would be left in my memory and I wouldn't think of her or remember her as someone who had been sent to my office for doing something against the school rules. It worked, the tears and words started simultaneously. I especially knew it worked, when after we had decided on the punishment, she turned as she left the room to ask if my memory problem had kicked in yet!

What is this all about? Girls, especially:

■ respond to disciplinary issues with the moral orientation of connectedness and caring: Lois needed to know that two adults (in this case the teacher and the director) that she cared about would not think she was a terrible person because of what she had done

■ will learn to be secretive if they hear consistently that they should be "good girls" that never do anything inappropriate

■ will stop translating their anger or frustration into more appropriate and healthier behavior if they are *only* punished and not guided to find direct ways of communicating their concerns

Understanding how this translates into the three C's paradigm is also important for parents. Lois walked out with improved confidence: she could handle a very difficult situation. Our discussion of talking to Mrs. Carr directly or writing a note to her about her anger gave her additional competence to handle future bouts of anger or frustration. Her feelings of connectedness and caring, which started out as a hindrance for telling the truth, was adjusted to show her how it could be part of being trusted and respected even if she did something with which the world did not agree. Strudel theory: if parents and other significant adults keep in mind the layering of the three C's during experiences of discipline, a very healthy strudel will be the end result. Once is not enough, luckily children keep making mistakes so that it seems that we have more than adequate opportunities to respond with guiding as the major component of discipline and punishment as a needed, but minor, component.

A second major crucible event is risk-taking. In this case, Lauren is our instructor:

Gymnastics is an important part of our P.E. curriculum throughout the lower school years because of its effects on positive body image, control, muscle development, movement through space, etc. One of our fourth graders, Lauren, has been trying to do a cartwheel into a backwards somersault in the air since she was in first grade — a difficult move for any elementary school child. One of the challenges for Lauren is that she is not as lithe as most gymnasts. But every year, when the gymnastics unit started, she would take out her portfolio and write down her goal for the year — a backwards mid-air somersault. Each year she would work so hard, each year she would come a bit closer. Her teachers and her peers cheered her on, never made fun of her, always applauded her increments of improvement.

Fourth grade is the last year in the primary division. The gymnastics unit ends in a show for all of the primary parents and students. Each fourth grader can choose to design and to perform her own gymnastics routine. You guessed it, Lauren chose to do a routine and had a part at the end of it where she went to the corner of the full floor mat and ran catty-corner across it, and at the midsection of the mat would spin a cartwheel and leap into the air with the somersault as the final component. I had missed seeing the rehearsal where Lauren had completed everything correctly except the somersault. Therefore, when Lauren went to the mat to start her routine and was waiting for the music to start, I had no idea why the tension in the room was palpable, why Miss Wilson (her P.E. teacher for the past four years) was leaning forward, why every other fourth grade girl sat bolt upright. The routine was very nice, Lauren was obviously giving it her "all." I thought it was merely her way of doing a good job, ending her primary gymnastics' stint, so to speak. Then, the music had a brief pause, Lauren stood poised at the end of the mat, the music started, she started running across the mat, she went up in the air, the entire fourth grade and Miss Wilson went up in he air, too. Lauren did the somersault in mid air and came down with a perfect landing. I was startled when thirty-five fourth graders and one PE teacher all screamed "Yes!" simultaneously and then proceeded to rush to the center of the gym, and, with no words or planning, lifted Lauren on their shoulders and carried her around the gym.

It wasn't until the teary Miss Wilson came back to tell us the background story that we understood what we had witnessed. Later that day, at lunch, I explained to Lauren why she was one of my role models, because she never gave up trying to do something that mattered to her, even though it was very difficult. At the end of the year, she wrote me a note that said that "her heart had filled up like a balloon" when everyone screamed yes and when I told her that she was one of my role models and that she would never forget that day, ever, no matter how long she lived.

Important components of this experience, layered over four years:

■ No one ever said to her that this might be too hard, that she might want to try a somersault on the ground, or that her body was not best designed for a somersault in flight.

■ She felt supported, not deflated when she was not able to meet her goal.

■ The goal was not set for Lauren by someone else.

■ She was taught how to break up this skill into its component parts and to master each part over time. An important component of this was a video camera that all of the girls used to tape their work and to sit and to critique it with their peers and teachers after each class.

■ Her parents supported her gymnastics dream by paying for gymnastics lessons even though they knew she would never go to the Olympics as a gymnast.

Competence and confidence are intricately connected to high expectations under conditions of great nurturing and support. What is sometimes called pejoratively "the Little League" parent is the obverse of this: someone who sets the bar very high, minus the nurturing conditions. This is often at the root of the issue when Olympic hopeful female athletes burn out and quit at a very young age. As the research would predict, high expectations without support is more of a deleterious situation for females than males. The connectedness factor is also fairly apparent in this story. Lauren may have been literally lifted into the air by her colleagues *after* the somersault, but their connectedness to her and hers to them helped lift her figuratively into the air *for* the somersault.

Crucible event #3 is related to how we deal with loss or separation. There are many examples in this category that really move along a continuum from the separation of a preschooler from a parent during the first stages of a school experience, to the divorce of parents, to the death of a beloved parent and all of the permutations and combinations in between these two examples. Irene's story has taught all of us a great deal about the more traumatic end of this continuum.

It's hard for us to remember, as adults, what is joyous about being a seven year old, until you spend time with a seven year old like Irene. She would burst through the front door of the school and beg to be allowed to go to her classroom early because "Mrs. G." was waiting for her. And, it was true, Mrs. G., her second grade homeroom teacher, like all of Irene's homeroom teachers through the years (she had been at the school since she was three), often encouraged her to come to the classroom early because she filled it with such energy and excitement and movement and chatter. What a way for any teacher to start the day!

So, it was with terrible pain and sadness that winter that we began to have meetings to talk about how to be supportive to Irene, her family, and all of us at Laurel who had become her extended family. Her mother was getting close to ending her battle with cancer, an end that would leave Irene without the presence of her mother in this world. The first faculty meeting was one of "shoulds." We *should* make sure she meets with our school psychologist so that she could talk about her feelings. We *should* make sure that she can go to the nurse at any time. We *should* make sure that she was relieved from doing her homework and did not feel pressure about what she had to learn at school. We *should* send a note home to the other parents in the class so that when Irene went to their homes for play days that they would know. The list went on. It was a very useful first meeting. It lead to our thinking through, as a school, how best to respond to this crucible event in the life of a child in a way that not only was supportive, but also helped the child to face future life a bit stronger. That's when we threw the above "shoulds" out of one of the school windows and began another conversation.

Irene's mother would only talk with Mrs. G.; luckily they had been friends before Irene was born. That formed our first guideline: Irene's mother could not handle talking to many people, including the director of the lower school, so Mrs. G. was the communication liaison. The next step was to talk to Irene and her father, to see how best to proceed to be what they needed. Dad asked for some reading materials. Irene asked that her school day be untouched: that her school remain a safe place where not many people knew about her mother's deteriorating condition, that no one talk to her with a tone of sympathy, that no exceptions for schoolwork be made for her, and that she did not want to talk to our psychologist. We learned a great deal that year.

After Irene's mother died, we talked with all of the second graders about how Irene wanted us to act when she came back to school. We also shared with the girls traditional psychological wisdom about how to express their thoughts and feelings to Irene with letters that she could read outside of school where she had the time and space to deal with them, but not to talk to her about this topic at school, unless Irene initiated it. We met with parents of her friends to have the same conversation. All of this happened with the permission and approval of Irene's dad, but not with Irene's knowledge. Her family felt strongly that it would bother Irene if she knew, at that time, that we were talking about her and her grief with her friends and their families.

Two years later, Irene's father remarried and they had plans to move to a new house. We learned even more from Irene's stepmother. She came in to talk about how best to help Irene with the transition of moving from where she had been raised, in a home decorated and lived in by her mother, to a new place. We talked about the importance of consulting with Irene and asking her if taking part of her home and her mother to her new home was important to her. It was. Irene's new home has the flowers lining the driveway, all the way up to the front door, that Irene's mother had planted at her previous house. They were lovingly dug up and transferred by Irene and her stepmother.

There is no blueprint for responding to death and dying, an incredible crucible event in the life of a child. Each needs to be designed somewhat individually. Irene has grown, physically and emotionally — she is about to enter fifth grade. What are the salient features of how things were handled?

■ There is little traditional wisdom and we need to be very careful not to impose our emotional needs or psychological history on the situation. That's what the first faculty meeting was all about. This was exceedingly difficult for the adults in her life.

■ Competence is a key factor — Irene needed to have part of her life with untouched expectations so that she could continue to perform and to be normal. Again, the first reaction of the adults in her life was to lower the bar, so to speak, to make things easier for her. It would have made things so much harder.

■ There are a plethora of connectedness factors in the above story. Irene's connectedness to the school and to her teacher played a huge role in maintaining a healthy path through this time period. It was the relationships that were important. At some points, this became confusing as adults and other children tried to use the material world to assuage Irene's pain — buying her wonderful presents, constantly taking her places or doing things so she wouldn't think about her mother.

■ Connectedness and competence are interrelated factors in terms of Irene being consulted about her needs and then helping to design the process. There is also a limit to this, as shown by our decision to talk to Irene's friends, even though we knew that she would have vetoed this decision.

■ All of the above ended in the increasing competence of Irene and her family to cope with pain and loss and will be translated to her increasing capability to handle future crucible events and moments in her life.

Crucible event #4 falls into the general category of change. This obviously can be related to and interactive with loss and separation, but there are also enough events in this category to warrant a separate story. Enter Abbey:

Abbey's parents made an appointment to talk about whether or not Abbey should come to our school in September, even though they had already signed a contract and paid their deposit. Mom patiently explained that although Abbey was only four years old, she had experienced eight major changes in those four years, including several geographic, school, house, and family pattern changes. She was presently attending an area nursery school, where she could remain next year, but the family was so impressed with our school, that when an opening occurred, they jumped. They were now having second thoughts, especially since their pediatrician had just told them that a great deal of change was very stressful for children. Their question — should they keep her at her present school to reduce the amount of change in her life, or should they move her to our school in September, where they hoped she would stay until graduation from high school.

I asked them to describe Abbey to me. What followed was the story of a beloved child who had loving parents, a safe and consistent home environment (although the actual physical structures changed a bit!), a nurturing and interesting school environment (although, again, there had been a few different ones!), and no evidence of symptoms of stress. Abbey laughed a lot, looked forward to going to school, liked people and talked easily to strangers, slept well, ate well. Mom talked about all of the things she and her husband had done to help with transitions and to keep connections. Abbey had pictures of all of the schools and houses she had lived in, she called the children from her previous neighborhoods, her bedroom in each new house had the same furniture and the walls were painted the color of Abbey's choice (which they planned and talked about before each move).

Without really knowing how or why, Abbey's parents had the wisdom and intuition to deal with the *how* of these crucible events in ways that were growth producing. They had layered these experiences in such a way that Abbey had become an adaptive and competent human who valued her past, present, and future connections. I explained that it was not the quantity or the timing of change that was "bad" for children, but how it was structured and handled. In their case, it really didn't matter whether Abbey stayed at her preschool or came to our school; they had created the layering of the filo dough so that they were going to have a healthy strudel no matter which choice they made.

This crucible event underscores so clearly that there are no experiences in and of themselves that are all bad or all good. It

isn't the *what* in terms of human development, it is the *how*. Change
is not bad. Change handled ineffectively is bad. Abbey's parents
thought about how to make sure that her three C's would be
enhanced by all of the changes in her life. She was incredibly connected to her parents, who stayed a constant in the midst of all of
the other external changes in her life. She obviously felt safe and
comfortable enough because of this to learn how to meet and to
interact with new people, thereby steadily increasing her competence
and confidence slowly over time. Abbey's parents also used tricks
of the psychological trade such as making her bedroom look and
feel alike regardless of the city in which it may have been located.

One caveat needs to be added here. Abbey also had the good for-
tune to have a temperament that allowed her to benefit from her
parents good sense and planning. There are some children who are
born with a temperament that immediately rails against any quantity
of change, no matter how well it is handled. But we can't negate
the importance of how change is handled just because an atypical
exception exists in the continuum of human nature.

Crucible category #5 revolves around issues of friendship. As you
are well aware by now, friendship is a critical component in the lives
of most females, and, therefore, often creates a plethora of crucible
events/moments. How we handle this as wise adults in the lives of
developing girls is the gist of Dana and Molli's story:

Dana and Molli had been so conscientious all year, and they truly
loved their teacher, Miss Crissman, so they gave all of their academic
tasks their best efforts. But once they started to become friends and
to spend time together, things changed. Their interest in each other
seemed to supersede schoolwork. Some assignments weren't completed on time. Dana and Molli were found in the rest room talking
and giggling instead of being on time for science class.

They almost made it through to summer without any serious
incidents. But then, with six days to go, Miss Crissman escorted
both Dana and Molli to my office. Their offense was making fun
of another classmate (who had a newly acquired bump on her
nose due to an accident) and causing that classmate to cry.

I asked Miss Crissman to leave and, uncharacteristically, began to share my disappointment with their recent behavior without listening to a word they had to say. (Uncharacteristically is a word I want very much to be true). I then said I needed to think about this and sent them on their way. Afterwards, I watched them march down the hall, muttering all the way, "it's not fair," meaning of course that how I handled this situation was not fair. It is so hard on adults when children are right and we are wrong.

Later that day, I called the girls' mothers to let them know why their daughters might come home and say that they were sent to the director's office. Dana's mother listened very politely and intently to what happened. And then she had what can be described as a typical knee-jerk parental reaction. She said that Dana had invited Molli for a play day that weekend and she would cancel that event, since, obviously, the interactive nature of their friendship was causing both of them to behave inappropriately and therefore, this was not a "positive friendship."

This elicited the going-against-the-grain spiel. I explained that there is a very important process in social development which is critical for us as adults to try not to be tempted to interfere with or to control. Girls of this age need the freedom to sample friendships, trying different sizes, types, intensities, and flavors — a bit like trying all of Baskin Robbins' thirty-one flavors of ice cream before knowing which flavor is the best.

"It is important to make mistakes at a fairly early age and to choose some pretty yucky flavors," I went on. "If we're lucky girls will make choices early in life that result in things like being sent to the director's office. If they make 'poor' choices later, it could result in much worse consequences like becoming pregnant or taking drugs. If parents try to control the alternatives for friendships early, only allowing play dates with sterling friendship options, girls will not learn about the diversity of human nature and the best fit for them in terms of a more lasting relationship." By the time we finished our conversation, Dana's mother was thanking her lucky stars that Dana wanted to spend time with Molli on Saturday and thought whoever suggested that she cancel that date with Molli was "too dumb to live." There's that phrase again.

Back to the drawing board with Molli and Dana. Both came to my office, at my invitation, the next day to hear what the consequences would be for their actions. This time I asked them to tell me their version of what had happened. They began by denying vehemently that they premeditatedly hurt the feelings of the owner of the bicycle-accident induced lumpy nose. Instead "lumpy nose" was telling the story and laughing about it herself and they just joined in, but would not have wanted to hurt her feelings — she was a friend! To the other charges, they pleaded guilty, acknowledging that their new friendship was sometimes more fun and seemingly more important than school work and being on time to science class. So they promised never to let their interaction interfere with their school focus again and were ready for the dire consequences of their delinquent actions. I told them that I had talked to their parents, and the only consequences would be those dictated by their parents at home. This time they were quiet on the way back to their classroom. My bet is that they were wondering how quickly I had changed to a fair director, or better yet, a director who is fair!

Crucible moments around friendships and relationships and the world's reaction to them (especially the significant adults) are a critical foundation for girls' development. As the research suggests, relationships form the bedrock of self-esteem for most females. This is not bad or good, it just is. Allowing girls to form relationships without too many adult parameters early on enhances their ability to develop a sense of confidence and competence to make choices about people and decisions about their behavior.

The five big crucible events will probably happen to everyone at sometime in her/his life, regardless of age. However, the above stories relate to young or preadolescent girls for a reason: these truly are the formative years, and early crucible events have a lifetime effect. There are many stories that could be told about older girls or women, but it is the events that occur up through adolescence that need to be underscored in terms of their impact on the developing human.

A crucible moment is more serendipitous, and to some extent, more trivial. However, as you have come to see the layering of the strudel over time with these less-than-earth-shattering-moments is the substance of each person's strudel (whereas one could say that the crucible events are the filling!) An example of a crucible moment is one that could be labeled: Oh you poor baby, i.e. dealing with the garden variety daily emotional pain:

Liz is five, hardly two-feet tall, big blue eyes, still having some developmental trouble with her L's and R's, which has the perceivable effect on adults of their saying, "Isn't she cute?" She was visiting her aunt in Ohio, and had just arrived at my house, sans squirt gun, which she was asked to bring. In addition to Liz, also present was her nine-year-old brother (Steve) and three other boys (Adam, David, and Kevin) who were children of another friend.

Before Steve and Liz's arrival, the play rules had been set for this ninety degree day in July. Everyone had a squirt gun and the gazebo was the safe space, only the gazebo. Liz stepped out of the gazebo before the rules were explained to her. She was promptly, consistently, and accurately squirted. She screamed and ran back to the gazebo making those heartbreaking child sobby noises. We are so programmed as caring adults to respond to the physical or emotional pain of small living things, so her Aunt Diana's response of taking Liz into her lap and wrapping her arms around her was not surprising behavior at all. But the next part was — she told Liz to come over and to talk to me about what to do.

Luckily, there was an unattached squirt gun on the table. "Liz," I said, "you can stay here in the gazebo and be unsquirted, or you can take the squirt gun and go back out into the yard with the other children." She opted for the squirt gun; I guess you can't always tell a book by its cover. "Would you like me to fill the squirt gun with regular water or very cold water," I asked. "Very cold water," was her answer. As she stepped out of the gazebo, she mumbled, "Prepare to die!" to no one in particular. The next screams were not from Liz.

Although neither of her parents were present for this crucible moment, how parents and other adults respond to the pain of a child is absolutely critical in the forging of self. Key factors include:

■ While acknowledging pain and providing a cuddly lap space is important, it is not enough, and if it is the only response, can lead to forging a child that becomes weaker, not stronger. However, the nurturing response is certainly a critical and needed component. This reminds me to say again, even though the basic tenet appears elsewhere, the magical blend of nurturing and challenging is the most healthy mix for the developing human, at any age.

■ Choices, choices, choices. This word cannot be stressed enough. It is up to the adult to help identify some choices, because the age or life experiences of children is not always such that they can see all of the viable choices in front of them. It is what my grandfather meant when he said, "Too late smart," referring to the wisdom accumulated over time and with experience. In the above example, it would have been even better if Liz had been asked if she could think of any other alternatives.

■ The components of confidence, competence, and connectedness in the above story should be quite apparent to the reader by now.

We make mistakes as adults in the lives of children and do not always behave or help children to behave with wisdom and strength as end products. In addition, we cannot control all of the other human beings in the world and how they will respond to the crucible moments or events in the life of any child, or more importantly *my* child. Enter insurance policies. Insurance policies are ways of buffering children who do not have perfect parents, teachers, or lives from the trials and tribulations of life forging them into unhealthy humans, in comparison to those healthy children who have had every crucible moment or event handled perfectly.

An example of an insurance policy is what Mary Pipher refers to as the "north star" in her book, *Reviving Ophelia*. A north star is something that a child has in her life that is precious, that she can count on, that she is passionate about. Sometimes that is the horse for the passionate rider, or the violin for the committed musician, or the hours spent on e-mail talking to all of those Internet cyber-space buddies. So that, as Mary Pipher says, when the waters get rough in adolescence and I come home from school knowing I am a geek and that I will be the only one in the universe not going to the senior prom, I can go out to the stables and Mr. Ed still loves me. My north star, Mr. Ed, will be enough to hold me somewhat steady until a human Mr. Ed finally appreciates my worth. One caveat is in order — parents cannot choose or force a child to choose a particular north star. Parents can only provide a rich smorgasbord early on in life along with the encouragement, not to mention the cost of things like riding lessons with Mr. Ed and pray that a daughter finds her north star before her hormones kick into gear.

This brings us to the end of the book. Of course, I hope the end also marks the beginning of a new relationship with the girls in our care. I hope all readers take away with them the clear understanding that gender inequities still exist, that our traditional methods of operating schools have and still do contribute to these inequities. I want us to examine the ways in which we may be working against the needs of girls, despite our best intentions, and strive toward solutions. And I want us to consciously focus on building and maintaining the self-esteem of girls in all of our interactions, knowing that in doing so we can help them realize their full potential. This is, after all, what we want — to clarify and act on the best practices in education that will allow all girls (and boys) to thrive in this world.

It is the hope of all educators and parents. And it is well within our grasp.

Resources

Parent Readings:

Barchers, Suzanne I., ed. *Wise Women: Folk and Fairy Tales from Around the World.* Colorado: Libraries Unlimited, Inc., 1990.

Bingham, Mindy and Sandy Stryker. *Things Will Be Different for My Daughter: A Practical Guide to Building Her Self-Esteem and Self-Reliance.* New York: Penguin Books, 1995.

Cadoff, Jennifer Kintzing. "How to Raise a Strong Daughter in a Man's World." *McCall's,* February, 1992, 58.

Crawford, Susan Hoy. *Beyond Dolls and Guns: 101 Ways to Help Children Avoid Gender Bias.* New Hampshire: Heinemann, 1996.

Debold, Elizabeth, et al. *Mother Daughter Revolution: From Good Girls to Great Women.* New York: Bantam Books, 1994.

Douglas, Susan J. *Where the Girls Are: Growing Up Female with the Mass Media.* New York: Times Books, 1994.

Eagle, Carol J. and Carol Colman. *All That She Can Be.* New York: Simon & Schuster, 1993.

Elium, Jeanne and Don Elium. *Raising a Daughter: Parents and the Awakening of a Healthy Woman.* California: Celestial Arts, 1994.

Girls Can: Community Coalitions Project. Washington D.C.: American Association of University Women Educational Foundation, 1996.

Godfrey, Joline. *No More Frogs to Kiss: 99 Ways to Give Economic Power to Girls.* New York: Harper Collins, 1995.

Gurian, Michael. *The Wonder of Boys: What Parents, Mentors, and Educators Can Do to Shape Boys into Exceptional Men.* New York: G.P. Putnam and Sons, 1996.

Katz, Montana. *The Gender Bias Prevention Book: Helping Girls and Women to Have Satisfying Lives and Careers.* New Jersey: Jason Aronson Inc., 1996.

Kelly-Benjamin. *The Young Women's Guide to Better SAT Scores: Fighting the Gender Gap.* New York: Bantam Books, 1990.

Kopecky, Gini. "The Age of Self-Doubt." *Working Mother,* July, 1992, 46-49.

Laskin, David and Kathleen O'Neill. *The Little Girl Book: Everything You Need to Know to Raise a Daughter Today.* New York: Ballantine Books, 1992.

Lloyd, Barbara and Gerard Duveen. *Clever Gretchen and Other Forgotten Folktales.* New York: Thomas Y. Crowell, 1980.

Mann, Judy. *The Difference:Growing Up Female in America.* New York: Warner Books, 1994.

McLoone, Margo and Alice Siegel. *The Information Please Girls' Almanac.* New York: Houghton Mifflin Company, 1995.

New Moon: The Magazine for Girls and Their Dreams, Duluth, Minnesota: Published Bi-monthly.

Odean, Kathleen. *Great Books for Girls.* New York: Ballantine Books, 1997.

Orenstein, Peggy. *Schoolgirls.* New York: Doubleday, 1994.

Phelps, Ethel Johnston. *The Maid of the North: Feminist Folk Tales from Around the World.* New York: Henry Holt and Company, 1981.

Pipher, Mary. *Reviving Ophelia: Saving the Selves of Adolescent Girls.* New York: G.P. Putnam's Sons, 1994.

Sadker, Myra and David. *Failing at Fairness: How America's Schools Cheat Girls.* New York: Charles Scribner's Sons, 1994.

Silverstein, Olga and Beth Rashbaum. *The Courage to Raise Good Men.* New York: Penguin Books, 1994.

Tannen, Deborah. *You Just Don't Understand: Women and Men in Conversation.* New York: Ballantine Books, 1990.

Thurber, James. *Many Moons.* New York: Harcourt Baace & Company 1943.

White, Kate. *Why Good Girls Don't Get Ahead But Gutsy Girls Do.* New York: Warner Books Inc., 1995.

Wilbur, Jessica. *Totally Private And Personal: Journaling Ideas for Girls and Young Women.* Minneapolis, Minnesota: Free Spirit Publishing Co., 1996.

Wilcox, Tom. "Not For Boys Only: Athletics Provide a Father-Daughter Bond." *Independent School,* Fall 1996.

A CONCISE SURVEY OF THE CURRENT RESEARCH AND MATERIALS ON GENDER

Aburdene, Patricia and John Naisbitt. *Megatrends for Women.* New York: Villard Books, 1992.

Achieving Gender Equity in the Classroom and On the Campus: The Next Steps. American Association of University Women, 1995.

Akin, Terri, et al. *The Best Self-Esteem Activities: For the Elementary Grades.* California: Innerchoice Publishing, 1990.

Allard, Andrea and Jeni Wilson. *Gender Dimensions: Developing Interpersonal Skills in the Classroom.* Australia: Eleanor Curtain Publishing, 1995.

Avery, Caryl S. "Voyage to Womanhood." *New Woman,* November, 1991.

Barbieri, Maureen. *Sounds from the Heart: Learning to Listen to Girls.* New Hampshire: Heinemann, 1995.

Barchers, Suzanne I. *Wise Women: Folk and Fairy Tales from Around the World.* Colorado: Libraries Unlimited, Inc., 1990.

Barrs, Myra and Sue Pidgeon. *Reading the Difference: Gender and Reading in Elementary Classrooms.* Maine: Steinhouse Publishers, 1993.

Begun, Ruth Weltmann, ed. *Ready to Use: Social Skills Lessons and Activities for Grades 4-6.* New York: The Center for Applied Research in Education, 1996.

"Beyond Beijing: Who's Doing What to Turn Words Into Action. " *Issues Quarterly,* Vol. 2 (1). Fall/ Winter 1996.

Bingham, Mindy and Sandy Stryker. *Things Will Be Different for My Daughter: A Practical Guide to Building Her Self-Esteem and Self-Reliance.* New York: Penguin Books, 1995.

Bird, Stephanie. *Mentoring Means Future Scientists: A Guide to Developing Mentoring Programs Based on the AWIS Mentoring Project.* Washington, D.C.: Association for Women in Science, 1993.

Blais, Madeleine. *In These Girls, Hope Is a Muscle.* New York: The Atlantic Monthly Press, 1995.

Bogart, Karen. *Solutions That Work: Identification and Elimination of Barriers to the Particpation of Female and Minority Students in Academic Educational Programs.* Professional Standards and Practice, National Education Association.

Borba, Michele. *Esteem Builders: A K-18 Self Esteem Curriculum for Improving Students Achievement: Behavior and School Climate.* Torrance, California: Jalamar Press, 1989.

"Boys and Girls/ Together and Apart." *Independent School,* Fall 1992.

Brandt, Ronald S. *Cooperative Learning and the Collaborative School.* Virginia: Association for Supervision and Curriculum Development, 1991.

Breecher, Deborah and Jill Lippitt. *The Women's Information Exchange National Directory.* New York: Avon Books, 1994.

Brown, Loulou, et al., eds. *The International Handbook of Women's Studies.* New York: Harvester Wheatsheaf, 1993.

Brown, Lyn Mikel and Carol Gilligan. *Meeting at the Crossroads: Women's Psychology and Girls' Development.* Massachusetts: Harvard University Press, 1992.

Butler, Kathleen A. *Learning Styles: Personal Exploration and Practical Applications.* Connecticut: The Learner's Dimension, 1995.

Byrne, Eileen M. *Women and Science: The Snark Syndrome.* Pennsylvania: The Falmer Press, 1993.

Cadoff, Jennifer Kintzing. "How to Raise a Strong Daughter in a Man's World." *McCall's,* February, 1992.

Canfield, Jack and Harold Clive Wells. *100 Ways to Enhance Self-Concept in the Classroom,* Second Edition. Massachusetts: Allyn and Bacon, 1994.

Campbell, Patricia B. *Girls Are...Boys Are...Myths, Sterotypes and Gender Differences.* Newton, Massachusetts: WEEA Resource Center, 1996.

Caplan, Paula J. *Lifting A Ton of Feathers: A Woman's Guide to Surviving in the Academic World.* Toronto: University of Toronto Press, 1993.

Chapman, Anne. *A Great Balancing Act: Equitable Education for Girls and Boys,* Washington, D.C.: National Association of Independent Schools, 1997.

Clair, Renee. *The Scientific Education of Girls: Education Beyond Reproach?* Pennsylvania: Jessica Kingsley Publishers Ltd., 1995.

Cohen, Judy, et al. *Girls in the Middle: Working to Succeed in School.* Washington, D.C.: American Association of University Women Educational Foundation, 1996.

Conwell, Catherine and Kitty B. Cobb, et al. *Science EQUALS Success.* Massachusetts: WEEA Publishing Center, Education Development Center, Inc., 1990.

Cooney, Miriam P., ed. *Celebrating Women in Mathematics and Science.* Reston, Virginia. National Council of Teachers of Mathematics.

Cotera, Martha P. *Checklists for Counteracting Race and Sex Bias in Educational Materials.* Austin, Texas: Women's Educational Equity Act, U.S. Department of Education, 1982.

Countryman, Joan. *Writing to Learn Mathematics: Strategies That Work, K-12.* New Hampshire: Heinemann, 1992.

Crawford, Susan Hoy. *Beyond Dolls & Guns: 101 Ways to Help Children Avoid Gender Bias.* New Hampshire: Heinemann, 1996.

Debold, Elizabeth, et al. *Mother Daughter Revolution: From Good Girls to Great Women.* New York: Bantam Books, 1994.

Douglas, Susan J. *Where the Girls Are: Growing Up Female with the Mass Media.* New York: Times Books, 1994.

Downie, Diane and Twila Slesnick and Jean Kerr Stenmark. *Math for Girls and Other Problem Solvers.* California: EQUALS, University of California, 1981.

Duff, Carolyn S. and Barbara Cohen. *When Women Work Together,* Berkley, California: Conari Press, 1993.

Eagle, Dr. Carol J. and Carol Colman. *All That She Can Be.* New York: Simon & Schuster, 1993.

Education for All: Women and Girls Speak Out on the National Education Goals. National Coalition for Women and Girls in Education.

Elium, Jeanne and Don Elium. *Raising a Daughter: Parents and the Awakening of A Healthy Woman.* California: Celestial Arts, 1994.

Exploring Works: Fun Activities for Girls. Newton, Massachusetts: Education Development Center, Inc., 1996.

Faddis, Bonnie and Patricia Ruzicka, Barbara Berard, Nancy Huppertz. *Hand in Hand: Mentoring Young Women: Guide for Planning, Implementing, and Evaluating a Mentoring Program, Book One.* Massachusetts: WEEA Publishing Center, Education Development Center, Inc., 1988.

____*Hand in Hand: Mentoring Yound Women: Ideabook for Mentors, Book Two.*
Massachusetts: WEEA Publishing Center, Education Development Center,
Inc., 1988.

____*Hand in Hand: Mentoring Young Women: Student Career Journal, Book Three.*
Massachusetts: WEEA Publishing Center, Education Development Center,
Inc., 1988.

Fennema, Elizabeth and Lilah Leder. *Mathematics and Gender.* New York:
Teachers College, Columbia University, 1990.

Flansburg, Sundra. *Center for Equity and Cultural Diversity Working Paper Two:
Building Self: Adolescent Girls and Self Esteem,* Massachusetts: WEEA
Publishing Center, Education Development Center, Inc., 1993.

Fort, Deborah C., ed. *A Hand Up: Women Mentoring Women in Science.*
Washington, D.C.: The Association for Women in Science, 1995.

Franck, Irene and David Brownstone. *Women's World: A Timeline of Women in
History.* New York: Harper Perennial, 1995.

Franklin, Margaret, et al. *Add-Ventures for Girls: Building Math Confidence:
Elementary Teacher's Guide.* Massachusetts: WEEA Publishing Center,
Education Development Center, 1990.

Gabriel, Susan L. and Isaia Smithson. *Gender in the Classroom: Power and
Pedagogy.* Illinois: University of Illinois Press, 1990.

Gaskell, Jane and John Willinsky. *Gender In/Forms Curriculum.* New York:
Teachers College Press, 1995.

Gender Equity: *Concepts and Tools for Development.* New York: The Center for
Development and Population Activities, 1996.

"Gender, Language and Literacy," *Language Arts,* Vol. 70, No. 2, February, 1993.

Genshaft, Judy and Jack Naglieri. *A Mindset for Math: Techniques for Identifying
and Working with Math-Anxious Girls.* Massachusetts: WEEA Publishing
Center, Education Development Center, Inc., 1987.

Gilligan, Carol. *In a Different Voice.* Cambridge, Massachusetts: Harvard
University Press, 19982.

Girls Can: Community Coalitions Project. Washington, D.C.: American Association
of University Women Educational Foundation, 1996.

Godfrey, Joline. *No More Frogs to Kiss: 99 Ways to Give Economic Power to Girls.*
New York: Harper Collins, 1995.

Gouchie, Catherine and Doreen Kimura. "The Relationship Between Testosterone
Levels and Cognitive Ability Patterns. "*Psychoneuroendocrinology,* Vol. 16,
No. 4, 1991.

Greenspan, Karen. *The Timetables of Women's History.* New York: Simon & Schuster, 1994.

Groothius, Rebecca Merrill. *Women Caught in the Conflict: The Culture War Between Traditionalism and Feminism.* Michigan: Baker Books, 1994.

Gurian, Michael. *The Wonder Boys: What Parents, Mentors and Educators Can Do to Shape Boys into Exceptional Men.* New York: G.P. Putnam and Sons, 1996.

Hallgarth, Susan A., ed. *Who's Where and Doing What: A Directory of the National Council for Research on Women.* New York: The National Council for Research on Women, 1993.
___and Tina Kraskow. *WIP: A Directory of Work-In Progress and Recent Publications.* New York: The National Council for Research on Women, 1992.

Hampson, Elizabeth and Doreen Kimura. "Brief Communication: Reciprocal Effects of Hormonal Fluctuations on Human Motor and Perceptual-Spatial Skills." *Behavioral Neuroscience,* Vol. 2, No. 3, 1988.

Hansen, Sunny and Joyce Walker and Barbara Flom. *Growing Smart: What's Working for Girls in School.* Washington, D.C.: American Association of University Women Educational Foundation, 1995.
___*Growing Smart: What's Working for Girls in School: Executive Summary and Action Guide.* Washington, D.C.: American Association of University Women Educational Foundation, 1995.

Hanson, Katherine. *Center for Equity and Cultural Diversity Working Paper One: Teaching Mathematics Effectively and Equitably to Females.* Massachusetts: WEEA Publishing Center, Education Development Center, Inc., 1992.

Harper, Timothy. "They Treat Girls Differently, Don't They?" *Sky,* December, 1996.

How Schools Shortchange Girls. American Association of University Women. 1992.

Hollinger, Debra and Rebecca Adamson. "Single-Sex Schooling: Proponents Speak." Vol. II, *A Special Report From the Office of Educational Research and Improvement,* U.S. Department of Education, 1992.

"How to Teach Our Kids." *Newsweek, Special Edition-Education: A Consumer's Handbook,* Fall/Winter, 1990.

Humphrey, Bernice. *What's Equal: Figuring Out What Works for Girls in Coed Settings.* New York: Girls Inc., 1992.

"In Search of the Mind." *Time,* July 7, 1995.

Invitation to Excellence: New Ideas for Teaching Mathematics and Science. Sponsored by Macmillan/McGraw-Hill and *Business Week.*

"Issues Involving Single-Gender Schools and Programs." *A Report to the Chairman*, Committee on the Budget, House of Representatives, May 1996.

Karnes, Frances A. and Suzanne M. Bean. *Girls and Young Women Leading the Way*. Minnesota: Free Spirit Publishing Inc., 1993.
___*Girls and Young Women Inventing*. Minnesota: Free Spirit Publishing Inc., 1995.

Katz, Lilian G. and Dinae E. McClellan. *The Teacher's Role in the Social Development of Young Children*. Illinois: ERIC Clearinghouse on Elementary and Early Childhood Education, University of Illinois, 1991.

Katz, Montana. *The Gender Bias Prevention Book: Helping Girls and Women to Have Satisfying Lives & Careers*. New Jersey: Jason Aronson Inc., 1996.

Kelly-Benjamin, Kathleen and Introduction by Phyllis Rosser. *The Young Women's Guide to Better SAT Scores: Fighting the Gender Gap*. New York: Bantam Books, 1990.

Kenway, Jane and Sue Willis. *Hearts and Minds: Self-Esteem and the Schooling of Girls*. New York: The Falmer Press, 1990.

Kerr, Barbara A. *Smart Girls Two: A New Psychology of Girls, Women and Giftedness*. Dayton, Ohio: Ohio Psychology Press, 1994.

Kimura, Doreen. "Are Men's and Women's Brains Really Different?" *Canadian Psychology*, 1987, 28:2.
___"Cognitive Function: Sex Differences and Hormonal Influences." *Neuroscience Year: Supplement 2 to the Encycolpedia of Neuroscience*, Birkhauser Boston, 1992.
___"How Different Are Male and Female Brains?" *Orbit*, Published by Ontario Institute for Studies in Education, Vol. 17, No. 3, October, 1986, 13-14.

___"Male Brain, Female Brain: The Hidden Difference." Reprinted from *Psychology Today*, November, 1985.

___"Monthly Fluctuations in Sex Hormones Affect Women's Cognitive Skills." *Psychology Today*, November, 1989.

___"Sex Difference, Human Brain Organization." *Encyclopedia of Neuroscience*, Vol. II, 1987.

Kopecky, Gini. "The Age of Self-Doubt." *Working Mother*, July, 1992.

Laskin, David and Kathleen O'Neill. *The Little Girl Book: Everything You Need to Know to Raise a Daughter Today*. New York: Ballantine Books, 1992.

Lawton, Millicent. "Bias Against Girls Found in Both Co-ed, One-Sex Schools." *Education Week*, June 10, 1992.

Leder, Gilah C. "Mathematics and Gender: Changing Perspectives." *Critical Issues.*

Lloyd, Barbara and Gerard Duveen. *Gender Identities and Education: The Impact of Starting School.* New York: St. Martin's Press, 1992.

Logan, Judy. *Teaching Stories.* St. Paul, Minnesota: Minnesota Inclusiveness Program, 1993.

Lurie, Allison. *Clever Gretchen and Other Forgotten Folktales.* New York: Thomas Y. Crowell, 1980.

Maher, Frances A. and Mary Kay Thompson Tetreault. *The Feminist Classroom: An Inside Look at How Professors and Students Are Transforming Higher Education for a Diverse Society.* New York: Basic Books.

Mann, Judy. "A Transformation Among Schoolgirls," *Washington Post,* June 1992.
___*The Difference: Growing Up Female in America.* New York: Warner Books, 1994.

Math & Science for Girls: Convening the Experts: Reforming the Classroom: Finding the Right Equation. The National Coalition of Girls' Schools, November, 1992.

McLone, Margo and Alice Siegel. *The Information Please Girls' Almanac.* New York: Houghton Mifflin Company, 1995.

"Mind and Brain." *Scientific American Special Issue,* Vol. 267, No. 3, September, 1992.

Morgan, Elaine, *The Descent of the Child.* New York: Oxford University Press, 1995.

Moussa, Farag. *Women Investors.* Switzerland: Farag Moussa, 1991.

Murphy, Susan H. "Closing the Gender Gap: What's Behind the Differences in Test Scores, What Can Be Done About It." *The College Board Review,* No. 163, Spring, 1992.

New Moon: The Magazine for Girls and Their Dreams. Duluth, Minnesota: Published Bi-Monthly.

Northrup, Christiane. *Women's Bodies, Women's Wisdom.* New York: Bantam Books, 1994.

Odean, Kathleen. *Great Books for Girls.* New York: Ballantine Books, 1997.

Opening the Gates for Women in Science. Journal of College Science Teaching, Vol. XXI, No. 5, March/April, 1992.

Orenstein, Peggy. *School Girls.* New York: Doubleday, 1994.

Overholt, Jim. *Math Wise!: Hands-On Activities and Investigations for Elementary Students.* New York: The Center for Applied Research in Education, 1995.

Perl, Terri. *Women and Numbers.* California: Wide World Publishing/Tetra, 1993.

Phelps, Ethel Johnston. *The Maid of the North: Feminist Folk Tales From Around the World,* New York: The Feminist Press, 1978.

Pipher, Mary. *Reviving Ophelia: Saving the Selves of Adolescent Girls.* New York: G.P. Putnam's Sons, 1994.

Porter, Nancy. *Women's Studies Quarterly: Women, Girls, and the Culture of Education,* Vol. XIX, No. 1 & 2, Spring/Summer, 1991, New York: Feminist Press.

"Profiles in Leadership." *Coalition Chronicle,* National Coalition of Girls' Schools, Vol. 1, Ed. 3.

Promoting Self-Esteem in Young Women: A Manual for Teachers. New York: The University of New York and the State Education Department Division of Civil Rights and Intercultural Relations, 1989.

Pross, Maureen N. "Do Women Care Too Much?" *New Cleveland Woman,* June, 1990.

Rayman, Paula and Belle Brett. *Pathways for Women in the Sciences: The Wellesley Report, Part One.* Massachusetts: Pathways Project, Center for Research on Women, 1993.

Riordan, Cornelius. *Girls and Boys in School: Together or Separate?* New York: Teachers College, Columbia University, 1990.

Rosser, Phyllis. *The SAT Gender Gap: Identifying the Causes.* Washington, D.C.: Center for Women Policy Studies, 1989.

Rubin, Donnalee. *Gender Influences: Reading Student Texts.* Illinois: Southern Illinois University Press, 1993.

Sadker, Myra and David. *Failing at Fairness: How America's Schools Cheat Girls.* New York: Charles Scribner's Sons, 1994.

Sanders, Jo. *Lifting the Barriers.* New York: Jo Sanders Publications, 1994.
____*The Neuter Computer: Computers for Girls and Boys.* New York: Neal-Schuman Publishers, Inc., 1996.

Schiebinger, Londa. *The Mind Has No Sex?: Women in the Origins of Modern Science.* Cambridge, Massachusetts: Harvard University Press.

Science: Women in Science. American Association for the Advancement of Science, Vol. 255, March, 13, 1992.

Science: Women in Science: Comparisons Across Cultures. American Association for the Advancement of Science, Vol. 263, March 11, 1994.

Science: Women in Science '93: Gender and Culture. American Association for the Advancement of Science, Vol. 260, April 16, 1993.

Secada, Walter G., et al., eds. *New Directions for Equity in Mathematics Education.* Cambridge University Press, 1995.

Sedgwick, John. "What Difference Does a Single-Sex School Make to a Girl Later in Life?" *Self Magazine,* March, 1997.

Siegel, Deborah L. *Sexual Harassment: Research and Resources.* New York: The National Council for Research on Women, 1992.

Silverstein, Olga and Beth Rashbaum. *The Courage to Raise Good Men.* New York: Penguin Books, 1994.

"Single-Sex Schooling: Perspectives From Practice and Research." Vol. I, *A Special Report From the Office of Educational Research and Improvement,* U.S. Department of Education (Draft as of December 22, 1992.)

Smith, Dian G. "Preschools Shortchange Girls." *Sesame Street Parents' Magazine,* September, 1992.

Sommerfield, Meg. "Foundations Respond to Critique of Girls' Education." *Education Week,* October 7, 1992.

Strategies for Success: What's Working in Education Today. Harvard Educational Review, President and Fellows of Harvard College, 1990.

Tannen, Deborah. *You Just Don't Understand: Women and Men in Conversation.* New York: Ballantine Books, 1990.

"The Confidence Quotient: Building Girls' Self-Esteem." *Keeping the Trust, A Quarterly Report from the Cleveland Foundation,* Summer, 1992.

"The New Science of the Brain." *Newsweek,* March 27, 1995.

The Scientific Education of Girls: Education Beyond Reproach? UNESCO. London: Jessica Kingsley Publishers, 1995.

The World's Women 1995: Trends and Statistics. New York: United Nations, 1995.

Thorne, Barrie. *Gender Play: Girls and Boys in School.* New Jersey: Rutgers University Press, 1993.

Thurber, James. *Many Moons.* New York: Harcourt Brace & Company, 1943.

Toufexis, Anastasia. "Coming from a Different Place." *Time,* Fall, 1990.

Trentacosta, Janet and Margaret J. Kenney. *Multicultural and Gender Equity in the Mathematics Classroom: The Gift of Diversity, 1997 Yearbook.* Virginia: The   National Council of Teachers of Mathematics, Inc., 1997.

Wade, Rahima Carol. *Joining Hands: From Personal to Planetary Friendship in the Primary Classroom.* Arizona: Zephyr Press, 1991.

Washington, Mary Ford. *Real Life Math Mysteries: A Kid's Answer to the Questions, "What Will We Ever Use This For?"* Texas: Prufrock Press, 1995.

Watson, Neil V. and Doreen Kimura. "Nontrivial Sex Differences in Throwing and Intercepting: Relation to Psychometrically-Defined Spatial Functions." *Person Indiv. Diff.,* Vol. 12, No. 5, 1991.

Weisbard, Phyllis Holman. *New Books in Women and Feminism.* Madison, Wisconsin: University of Wisconsin, Yearly Publication.

Wheeler, Kathryn. *Special Report: How Schools Can Stop Shortchanging Girls (and Boys): Gender-Equity Strategies: A Practical Manual for K-12 Educators, CRW6.* Massachusetts: Center for Research on Women, 1993.

White, Kate. *Why Good Girls Don't Get Ahead But Gutsy Girls Do.* New York: Warner Books Inc., 1995.

Wilbur, Jessica. *Totally Private and Personal: Journaling Ideas for Girls and Young Women.* Minneapolis, Minnesota: Free Spirit Publishing Co., 1996.

Wilcox, Tom. "Not For Boys Only: Athletics Provide a Father-Daughter Bond." *Independent School,* Fall 1996.

Willis, Scott Coop. "Learning Shows Staying Power." *Update: Association for Supervision and Curriculum Development,* Vol. 34, No. 3, March, 1992.

Willoughby, Stephen S. *Mathematics Education for a Changing World.* Virginia: The Association for Supervision and Curriculum Development, 1990.

Wilson, Meg. *Options for Girls: A Door to the Future, An Anthology on Science and Math Education.* Texas: Pro-Ed, 1992.

"Women: The Road Ahead." *Time Special Issue,* Vol. 136, No. 19, Fall, 1990.

Women's Studies Quarterly: Women, Girls, and the Culture of Education, Vol. 19, No. 1&2, Spring/Summer 1991, New York: The Feminist Press at The City University of New York.

Wrigley, Julia, ed. *Education and Gender Equaltiy.* London: The Falmer Press, 1992.

Young, Wathene. *A-Gay-Yah: A Gender Equity Curriculum for Grades 6-12.* Massachusetts: WEEA Publishing Center, Education Development Center, Inc., 1992.

ABOUT THE AUTHOR

JoAnn Deak is the director of the primary division at Laurel
School in Cleveland, Ohio. She earned her Ph.D. at Kent State
University specializing in preventive psychology and systems
intervention. She maintained a private practice until shortly after
she joined the faculty at Laurel School in 1978 where she first
served as school psychologist. A nationally recognized expert on
gender-related learning differences, Deak has addressed both
popular and professional audiences across the country.

58